PREEMPTING THE HOLOCAUST

The Holocaust and the Literary Imagination (1975)

The Age of Atrocity *Death in Modern Literature* (1978)

Versions of Survival *The Holocaust and the Human Spirit* (1982)

Holocaust Testimonies *The Ruins of Memory* (1991)

Admitting the Holocaust *Collected Essays* (1995)

Art from the Ashes *A Holocaust Anthology* (1995)

Landscapes of Jewish Experience *Paintings by Samuel Bak* (1997)

LAWRENCE L. LANGER

Preempting the Holocaust

Yale University Press   New Haven and London

Published with assistance from the foundation established
in memory of Philip Hamilton McMillan of the
Class of 1894, Yale College.

Designed by Sonia Scanlon
Set in Adobe Garamond type by Keystone Typesetting, Inc.
Printed in the United States of America
by BookCrafters, Chelsea, Michigan.

Library of Congress Catalog Number 98-60967
ISBN 0-300-07357-7

A catalogue record for this book is available from the
British Library.

The paper in this book meets the guidelines for
permanence and durability of the Committee on
Production Guidelines for Book Longevity of the
Council on Library Resources.

10 9 8 7 6 5 4 3 2 1

For Sandy

with thanks

for fifty blissful years

and more to come!

Contents

Acknowledgments

"Preempting the Holocaust" was first presented in 1996 as the keynote address at a Holocaust conference at the University of Notre Dame. "Legacy in Gray: The Ordeal of Primo Levi" was the keynote lecture in 1995 at an international conference on Primo Levi at the University of British Columbia. "Gendered Suffering: Women in Holocaust Testimonies" was published in Dalia Ofer and Leonore J. Weitzman, eds., *Women in the Holocaust* (Yale University Press, 1998). A different version was presented in 1995 at a conference on women and the Holocaust at Hebrew University, Jerusalem. "The Alarmed Vision: Social Suffering and Holocaust Atrocity" appeared in *Daedalus: Journal of the American Academy of Arts and Sciences* (Winter 1996) and is reprinted with permission. An earlier version was presented at a conference on social suffering at the Rockefeller Conference Center in Bellagio, Italy, whose director and staff I thank for their gracious hospitality. "Landscapes of Jewish Experience: The Holocaust Art of Samuel Bak" was published in *Landscapes of Jewish Experience: Paintings of Samuel Bak* (University Press of New England, 1997) and is reprinted together with illustrations with permission of the Pucker Gallery, Boston. An earlier version of "Two Holocaust Voices: Cynthia Ozick and Art Spiegelman" was presented in 1995 at a conference on American writers and the Holocaust at the United States Holocaust Memorial Museum in Washington, D.C. An earlier version of "The Stages of Memory: Parents and Children in Holocaust Texts and Testimonies" was presented in 1996 at an international conference on the work of Elie Wiesel in Stuttgart, Germany. "The Inner Life of the Kovno Ghetto" was published in *Hidden History of the Kovno Ghetto* (United States Holocaust Memorial Museum and Little, Brown, 1997) and is reprinted with permission. A briefer version of "*Undzere Kinder:* A Yiddish Film from Poland," was presented as a paper at the annual conference in Boston in 1995 of the Association for Jewish Studies. "Wiesenthal's *Sunflower* Dilemma: A Response" appears in this volume for the first time. "Opening Locked Doors: Reflections on Teaching the Holocaust" was published in *Dimensions: A Journal of Holocaust Studies* (9:2, 1995) and is reprinted with permission.

I am grateful to the conveners of the various conferences named above for their invitations and hospitality.

Introduction

The essays in this volume grow out of a restless discontent with the lingering habit of shifting the focus of Holocaust discussion from the central issue of mass murder to any number of auxiliary matters that skirt the question of how it was done, and why. The explosive controversy that greeted the publication of Daniel Goldhagen's *Hitler's Willing Executioners,* with its argument that the Germans and Austrians were driven principally by antisemitic hatred in their campaign to exterminate European Jewry, typifies the consternation that the topic still rouses. Some of the disagreement with Goldhagen's thesis seems justified; surely much of that animus was directed against non-Jews, too. As late as April 28, 1945, scarcely a week before the end of the war, the SS were still murdering *non-Jews* in the small gas chamber at Mauthausen. And that German wrath was aimed at Communists (to say nothing of other groups) as well as Jews is clear not only from Hitler's speeches but also from the behavior of the Einsatzgruppen on the eastern front. Moreover, this "hatred" was not confined to Germans and Austrians: anyone familiar with the ferocity of Lithuanians (in Kovno, for example), Latvians, Ukrainians, Romanians, and Croatians will understand that once official constraints were removed, other national groups could also proceed with the slaughter of Jews without inhibition.

Notwithstanding this, opposition has been raised to the very idea of hatred as a motive for the mass murder. The metaphor of a "killing machine" has found favor among many historians because it supports the idea of mass murder as a bureaucratic enterprise, bolstered by the image of industrial efficiency that dominates so much of twentieth-century thought. Although there is evidence to support this view, it must be qualified by the repeated breakdown of the killing facilities in a deathcamp like Belzec; by the flawed design of the mobile killing vans used at Chelmno and in Yugoslavia; by the initial failure of the brick in crematorium chimneys in Auschwitz; by the unreliability of engines from downed enemy planes as a source of carbon monoxide for the gas chambers at Treblinka; by the constant problem of the disposal and "redisposal" of bodies—leaving us with a mixed tale of "inefficient efficiency" as a designation for the German murder machinery. The very image of machinery rather than man as the primary instrument of liquidation tends to absolve individual offenders and obscure the identity *and* the catalyst of the very culprits who initiated and carried out the crime.

Whenever I read about the "machinery of death" during the Third Reich I am reminded of the innumerable acts of atrocity that witnesses recount in their testimony about their personal ordeals. It is easy to reconcile them with Goldhagen's idea of the driving force of hatred but difficult to square them with the notion of a bureaucratic or industrialized efficiency. These episodes of remembered ruthlessness are not exceptional instances of sadism or psychotic rage, and cannot be explained by peer pressure or careerism or the excuse of following orders. There is no need to rehearse the specific horrors here. As portrayed, they are deeds done not with a monumental indifference or casual brutality but with a savagery that can be explained only by a vindictive animosity against the victim. They are acts of unprovoked private fury, of what Primo Levi called excessive and needless cruelty that in some twisted yet psychologically understandable way may have been a source of spontaneous fulfillment to their agents. The reluctance among Goldhagen's detractors to accept this as a basic motive among the murderers curbs endeavors to locate the frontiers between guilt and innocence in this morally murky milieu.

At the end of *Ordinary Men,* his classic study of Police Battalion 101, Christopher Browning addresses the troubling issue of how a group of men who were not fanatic Nazis gradually adapted, whatever their initial reluctance, to the habit of killing Jews. Ultimately, they shot or sent to their death in Treblinka more than eighty thousand of them. Although he cites Primo Levi's description of a "gray zone" that dims ethical distinctions for both criminals and victims, Browning is careful to insist that Germans and Jews caught in this zone were not mirror images of each other: "those who killed cannot be absolved by the notion that anyone in the same situation would have done as they did." And yet he concludes his study with a paradoxical interrogative suggesting that anyone in the same situation *might* have: "If the men of Reserve Police Battalion 101 could become killers under such circumstances, what group of men cannot?" To the end of his life, Primo Levi was exasperated by theoretical questions such as this. Though Browning introduces his without prejudice of any sort, Levi could have replied with some asperity, as he does in *The Drowned and the Saved* to similar statements, "I do not know, and it does not much interest me to know, whether in my depths there lurks a murderer, but I do know that I was a guiltless victim and I was not a murderer." Levi would have maintained that the universalizing tendencies implicit in Browning's final inquiry dilute the charge of German evil by deflecting our attention from the crimes that some men committed to ones that others might have committed but did not. For Levi, such logic led toward a futile and irrelevant inquest into the realm of the possible that shed little light on actual incidents.

To intimate that we are all *potentially* complicit, by the affinity of our natures as human beings, in the kind of crime we call the

Holocaust is to overlook a fundamental difference that may not lead us any further toward insight than Browning's query does but at least discourages spurious comparisons—Browning himself, of course, is not guilty of this—with the widespread penchant for atrocity. The fact is that when ordinary men agree to mass murder, for *whatever* reasons, they cease to be ordinary men like the rest of us and assume the role of killers. At that point, Primo Levi would contend, any attempt to adjust the focus from their behavior to ours plays the game of evasion. It may be true, as Browning argues, that "everywhere people seek career advancement"; but the corollary does not necessarily follow that they do so by killing Jews. Once they have crossed that divide, they give us graver matters to consider than whether we would have done the "same" thing in their circumstances.

It is not difficult to understand the resistance to the radical change in our thinking required by an event like the Holocaust. This was brought home to me with special force by an encounter at a recent Passover seder with a *Hagadah* that included in its ritual celebration of the Jewish escape from Egypt a section lauding uprisings in the Warsaw and other ghettos (including Vilna, where none occurred) during the Holocaust. How we are to join the exodus of the Jews from slavery to freedom and the beginning of the journey to the Promised Land with the deportation of the Jews from freedom to slavery and certain death has never been obvious to me, but it illustrates the kind of detour that many of the essays in this volume try to explore. The *Hagadah* contains the poem "I Never Saw Another Butterfly," written by a child (later gassed in Auschwitz) in the Terezin ghetto. The editor notes in the text that it adds a touch of hope and grace to the story of the Holocaust. No one is coaxed to ask what hope and grace have to do with a historical episode that ended in mass murder or how it will help future generations who read this *Hagadah* to harmonize the successful liberation from Pharaoh with the fatal near-triumph of Hitler.

If I prefer the approach to this dilemma taken by Samuel Bak in his extraordinary series of paintings "Landscapes of Jewish Experience" (discussed in this volume), it is because Bak is candid enough to acknowledge that the Holocaust has introduced an inescapably somber strain into the story of the Jewish people. Himself a survivor of the Vilna ghetto, Bak insists on a tension rather than a union between the two narratives: a positive chronicle moving from Creation to Exodus and a desert journey under divine guidance to a safe destination; and a negative one, beginning with round-ups and finishing with train voyages to a perplexing abandonment and final doom. Without discarding the unquestionable value of Jewish tradition, Bak claims that its resonance has been altered by the modern narrative. In the "text" of his paintings, the Sabbath candle and the crematorium chimney are in ceaseless conflict, icons of reverence and disaster whose flames light up diverse if not totally unrelated worlds of remembering.

The shock that greeted the death of Primo Levi, many refusing to believe that he could have taken his own life, is another example of the unwillingness to allow for a painful and uneasy stress between trauma and recovery. The whole notion of "recovery" from the humiliation that Levi and others had to bear imagines the Holocaust as a treatable illness responsive to some kind of intellectual medication. A strain of melancholy, as I strive to show, runs through much of what Levi wrote, so that although one cannot call his suicide predictable, one might find it less surprising than many have appeared to do. Levi as a suicide demolishes the idea that he had mastered his past, come to terms with the atrocity of Auschwitz, and rejoined the human community healed and whole. Life went on for him, of course, though it is probably a mistake to think of his writing as a form of therapy, a catharsis that freed him from what he called the memory of the offense. It is clear from everything he wrote that survival did not mean a restored connection with what had gone before. The legacy of permanent disruption may be difficult to accept, but it lingers in his suicide like an abiding parasite.

King Lear's final words—"Look there, look there"—are an invitation to see continuity where only death prevails. His illusion, translated to the current predicament of facing the Holocaust, seems to represent a kind of genetic necessity that would enable the human species to endure such a comprehensive disaster undiminished and with the tapestry of hope intact. Perhaps the fault lies with attempts to read history as if it were tragedy. In most tragedy—*King Lear* may be a singular exception—some form of community survives to restore society's health after the evil has been exhausted; catharsis implies a healing process. Particular individuals may be destroyed, but the unity of life remains. What equivalent to the aesthetic pleasure some detect in tragedy, however, could be unearthed in the history of the Holocaust? The moral implication (if not "value") that one searches for in tragic drama is often carried over to the Holocaust by those who mistake tragedy for history. When asked if there were any meaning in the Holocaust, historian Raul Hilberg is said to have replied, "I hope not."

Whether tragedy is in fact "therapeutic," whether catharsis or a purgation of the emotions is one of its key ingredients, remains debatable. But some features of tragedy infiltrate Holocaust response when commentators seek among victims, as Tristan Todorov does, exemplars of heroic dignity to rescue from the anonymity of mass murder individual gestures of self-affirmation. Stage representation of suffering may induce a raw admiration; but history is unbearable in ways that mimesis is not. No matter how noble and praiseworthy the examples Todorov celebrates of "goodness" in the camps, they are surrounded by an ongoing catastrophe that private displays of compassion cannot pacify. To the illusion of "Look there, look there," we may reply with the reality of "Look here, look here." Unfortunately, history and theater are not convertible forms; I would go further and add that the idea of tragedy is utterly alien to Holocaust atrocity. The dignity of the one tells us nothing about the indignity of the other; efforts to identify the doom of the anonymous victim with the fate of the tragic figure can lead only to confusion.

The habit of using mass murder as a text for furthering personal agendas about humanity's capacity for goodness or its ability to resist oppression threatens to displace the original narrative of atrocity with a variety of alternative models. Educators who use the Holocaust to teach tolerance might well study a film like *Undzere Kinder* or Cynthia Ozick's Rosa stories or Art Spiegelman's *Maus* volumes (all discussed in these essays) to uncover the duress that makes this goal such a problematic one. Writers and intellectuals in Germany described the immediate postwar period as *Stunde Null*, Zero Hour, suggesting that the clock of civilization had returned to some primal moment when a drastic change of attitude would be necessary before any rebuilding of the future could be undertaken. History has shown how tiny the audience was for their neglected notion; in their own country, economic miracles overrode the cultural devastation, and there was little time or inclination to test the need or the capacity to mourn. The urgency to undo ruin has always outpaced the desire to confront it.

How to incorporate the Holocaust into our moral or historical intuitions about past *or* future remains a challenge to the modern intelligence. Mass murder impedes theories of progress, though advocates of progress seem to pay this little heed. In the absence of an authentic controlling myth to explain and enclose the Holocaust, its status drifts without social or artistic moorings. Unlike Dante, whose physical and spiritual journey changed a pilgrim into a poet with a comprehensive epic view that could portray and transcend the corruption of his time, the student of the Holocaust has no comparable hierarchic image to reflect its complexity. Although many commentators have used the descent into Hell as a parallel to the experience of Auschwitz, their zeal only betrays a misunderstanding of how Stunde Null had severed all such connections. To be sure Dante's Hell, like Milton's, is a place of torment, but that is the least important analogy. Its continued use only reveals how desperate we are to impose on the chaos of mass murder the "order" granted by antecedents.

For some, any conception may be better than none, if it responds to the inherent need for form. Despite the agonies it depicts, Dante's *Inferno* represents the essence of form. The gravest sinners are placed furthest from God, and each punishment reflects, indeed extends, the nature of the sin. Hell is retribution; there, justice prevails. But in Dante, the victims are also the sinners, while in Auschwitz they are not. Here, *in*justice prevails, and we are faced with the torment of the innocent. Any "ascent" is both ironic and grim, not a spiritual voyage but a fatal one. In other words, the Holocaust sabotages the dominant metaphor of hierarchy that has for so long characterized the moral and spiritual tone of our civilization and left us nothing with which to supplant it. If we hope to reestablish the principle of hierarchy by alleging dubious resemblances between Auschwitz and Hell, we only accentuate the instinct for rejuvenating exhausted modes of perception in the absence of creative replacements.

Perhaps Levi's gray zone has of necessity permeated Holocaust discussion more than we like to allow. Dante could draw on both classical and Christian precedents for the philosophical and theological structure of his *Commedia,* as well as an accessible Gospel style for the language of his verse. He could describe with graphic precision both the anguish of Hell and the bliss of Paradise because art is free to invent its own reality. Moreover, as Virgil never tires of reminding his untutored pupil, the rule of Heaven, the Will of an Other, reigns even amid the apparent disorder of Hell. But no such assurances are available to anyone either studying or trying to reimagine the origins and the consequences of the "Final Solution" or Nazi Germany's other killing schemes. Holocaust reality limits rather than liberates the vision of the writer, historian, or artist who ventures to represent it. It abnormalizes the normal, as in Claude Lanzmann's *Shoah,* where before our eyes the familiar train voyage metamorphoses into a journey toward death—without benefit of Virgil, or the divine guides who later displace him.

The closure of Dante's medieval epic has no parallel in the Holocaust, which leaves us only a legacy of spiritual vagueness and uncertainty to grapple with as we sort out its relevance to the morality of history and the history of morality. The purpose of these essays is to contribute to the incessant anxious dialogue about how our civilization may absorb into its reasonable hopes for the future the disabling outburst of unreason we name the Holocaust, as it continues to assault memory and imagination with immeasurable sorrow and undiminished force.

ONE

Preempting the Holocaust

The unshakable conviction that the Holocaust contains a positive lesson for all of us today unites the three figures whose ideas I plan to examine here. The intellectual, the artist, and the cleric, whom I will identify shortly, each unfolds a vision of that event consonant with his or her worldview. When I speak of preempting the Holocaust, I mean using—and perhaps abusing—its grim details to fortify a prior commitment to an ideal of moral reality, community responsibility, or religious belief that leaves us with space to retain faith in their pristine value in a post-Holocaust world.

Although I find this strategy both misleading and presumptuous, I have no corrective vision of my own to provide, other than the opinion that the Holocaust experience challenged the redemptive value of all moral, community, and religious systems of belief. A life more shrouded by darkness than radiant with light—one inevitable bequest of the mass murder of European Jewry—is not necessarily a hopeless one, but only the least sensitive among us could celebrate a return to absolute normalcy after such chaos. Indeed, another major legacy of that event is the defeat of the words that try to describe it, since after such *ab*normalcy our very definitions of the normal seem flaccid and weak, while a generic term like "chaos" cannot begin to portray the moral and spiritual anarchy of those grievous times.

Let me begin with a concrete detail, because I am convinced that all efforts to enter the dismal universe of the Holocaust must start with an unbuffered collision with its starkest crimes. Recently I was watching the testimony of a survivor of the Kovno ghetto. He spoke of the so-called *Kinderaktion,* when the Germans rounded up all the children (and many elderly) and took them to the nearby Ninth Fort for execution. The witness was present in the room when an SS man entered and demanded from a mother the one-year-old infant she was holding in her arms. She refused to surrender it, so he seized the baby by its ankles and tore the body in two before the mother's eyes.[1]

Whenever I hear stories like these, which unfortunately are not exceptional but illustrative of hundreds of similar incidents, I react with the same frozen disbelief, partly because of the intrinsic horror of the episode but also because it violates my sense of how life should and might be lived. I try to imagine the response of those in attendance—the mother, the witness, and the killer—but even more, I ask myself what we can do with such information, how we can inscribe it in the historical or artistic narratives that later will try to reduce to some semblance of order or pattern the spontaneous defilement implicit in such deeds? Where shall we record it in the scroll of human discourse? How can we enroll such atrocities in the human community and identify them as universal tendencies toward evil inherent in all humankind?

Well, we can't: we require a scroll of *in*human discourse to contain them; we need a definition of the *in*human community to coexist with its more sociable partner, and in their absence, we turn by default to more traditional forms of expression. The results may be comforting, but what price must we pay for such ease? The alternative is to begin by accepting a reality that escapes the bounds of any philosophy or system of belief that we have cherished since our beginnings, and to pursue the implications of this unhappy admission wherever they may lead. Consider, for example, this fragment of testimony from a former inmate of Auschwitz and Plaszow:

> We never knew . . . who would come back from roll call. Those who were "selected" for the "action" had to first dig their graves, then after stripping and placing everything they were wearing on the ground (in proper order: clothes on one side, underwear on the other), they had to kneel at the edge of the ditch and wait for the bullets in the back. Bullets that the Germans made the Jewish "leaders" of the camp pay for. Economizing on ammunition meant that the work was often botched, and cries rose from the ditches for hours after the execution. During large "actions" things moved too fast. There was no question of burying the bodies, they were simply covered with sand, so you could no longer tell whether you were walking on bones that were old or recent. Everything happened so fast that you didn't even have time to see your mother or sister vanish. We were no longer capable of suffering, or of being scared or surprised. Death is only frightening to the living. We hadn't been that for a long time.[2]

It is fearful enough to have to outlive the death, or more exactly the murder, of those one loves, some of whom have been buried while still breathing. But it is equally agonizing to have to outlive one's *own* death, as this witness insists she did, embracing an anguish beyond suffering that lifts her experience out of the realm of the familiar and deposits it in a limbo whose boundaries have yet to be clearly defined. We have the option of accepting the Holocaust as an event in quest of a concept to contain it or a language to express it, a phenomenon alien to our usual patterns of speech or belief; or we can assume that it only threatens but does not subvert the virtue, the vision, and the lovingkindness that my intellectual, my artist, and my cleric affirm. They do so as they venture to face the Holocaust with a universalizing vocabulary and imagery that never troubles to ask what it might mean to be dead while one was still alive. Which path we choose to follow depends on a complex tension between the stable instincts of our nature and a reality that tramples on those instincts with a contemptuous disdain.

"If we fail to master the past," writes Tzvetan Todorov in *Facing the Extreme: Moral Life in the Concentration Camps,* echoing both a famous German formulation and an overquoted aphorism of George Santayana, "it may master us." But it is not some abstract force called "the past" that the Holocaust challenges us to master; it is the mass murder of European Jewry. It is an SS man tearing a Jewish infant in two, or the German and Lithuanian murderers at the Ninth Fort in Kovno not even bothering to learn whether their victims were all dead before they ordered them to be covered with sand. How one goes about "mastering" such atrocities, as one of the murderers, or as a surviving member of the burial detail, or even as a detached reader today, I have no idea; I don't even know what "mastering" means in this context. But I suspect it doesn't help much to secrete such moments beneath a blanket of bland and evasive phrasing. *What* one faces when one faces the "extreme" of genocide is less important to Todorov than the assurance that moral life was still possible in the camps for both victims *and* murderers in spite of what went on there. He is not much interested in the specific agonies of the victims or the precise brutalities of their killers. He prefers instead to rescue both from the precincts of extremity and return them to the landscape of what he calls ordinary situations.

Todorov admits that many who outlived the camps and ghettos have written and spoken eloquently if bitterly about the selfish ways of behaving forced on them by the need to stay alive. But he is unwilling to accept this as a prevailing or even a requisite norm. It may seem odd that as recently as 1991 an intellectual as renowned as Todorov still finds it necessary to confirm the possibility of moral life even in the concentration camp (especially after Terrence Des Pres had defended the same idea so eloquently in *The Survivor* fifteen years earlier); I suppose, given the history of our indecent century, the impulse to defend the decency of the human species must surface periodically as ballast against the darker view.

But when such an effort is based on a dubious opposition between ordinary virtue on one hand and what Todorov calls "the principles of immorality expressed by the survivors" on the other, the resultant dichotomy leads us astray and blurs the tangled issue of who behaved how and why. Polarities, of which Todorov is unduly fond, quickly disintegrate in the atmosphere of a place like Auschwitz. For example, I have never heard a single survivor refer to the "principles of immorality" that governed his or her conduct in the camps. This locution is Todorov's invention, designed to strengthen a contrast between moral and immoral that may never have existed. He admits—and he really gives the game away through this admission—that "as a project, interpreting evil appeals less to me than understanding goodness."[3] As a result, he devotes most of his considerable intellectual energy to recovering the human, in both victims and their oppressors, from the midst of the inhuman, and then expanding the circle of those reassured to include his readers, and himself.

Todorov's book is one of three recent examples of universalizing the Holocaust that I am addressing in this inquiry. What happened in Nazi Germany and Stalin's Russia—Todorov speaks of them interchangeably—might have been done to, or done by, all of us. Experience, he says, is a contest between ordinary virtues—he labels them decency, caring, and the life of the mind—and ordinary vices—fragmentation, depersonalization, and the enjoyment of power. The Holocaust was little more than a drastic example of this modern conflict, and once we understand that, we will be in a better position to combat the totalitarian form of suppression of which the Holocaust was a not so singular example. This is a concise summary of Todorov's argument.

And where does all of this lead us—or lead Todorov? Well, it leads him to some extraordinary statements, and some even more extraordinary conclusions. Imagine their impact on the uninitiated reader, in search of authoritative accounts of the Holocaust. For example: "It is worth noting that the great majority of survivors have fallen victim to depression or trauma. The rate of suicide among this group is abnormally high, as is the prevalence of mental and physical illness." Or: "Life in the camps had been arduous in the extreme, and precisely because of this there had been something exalting in it [*elle a quelque chose d'exaltant*]. After the intensity of this experience, everything seemed colorless, futile, false" (263, 266). If the unexamined life is not worth living, what are we to say of these unexamined obiter dicta?

"Camp inmates," Todorov asserts—he seldom refers to Jews— "were made to know the far limits of human experience; it became their duty to humanity to report, in all honesty, what they saw and what they felt, for even in the most horrible experience there is some possibility for mankind's enrichment [*un enrichissement*]; only total oblivion calls for total despair." Because many victims were still alive at the end of the war, obviously we are not dealing with total oblivion. Hence the truth of their ordeal as they transmit it should not only enlighten and instruct but also enrich. One truth of their ordeal is as follows: A doctor at Mauthausen, in training as a physician for the front with an SS unit, liked to amputate the arms or legs of Jews to see how long it would take them to bleed to death. After all, this would be useful medical information for his subsequent military career. And once, when he was not thus professionally engaged, showing admirable initiative, because he clearly was not ordered to do this, he took two young

Jews from an arriving transport, killed them, cut off their heads, then boiled the flesh from the skulls, which he used as desk trophies for himself and a colleague. After the war, he married another doctor and together they set up a gynecological practice in Germany. How this confirms Todorov's theoretical conviction that even in the most horrible experience, there is some possibility for humankind's enrichment must forever remain a mystery to most of us—though in a gruesome sense, it does ratify his opinion that "no life is lived in vain if it leaves behind some trace of itself" (96).

I suppose anyone can excavate from the rubble of mass murder a piece of testimony to support his or her philosophy or system of belief or critical point of view. Many of us who explore the terrain of atrocity are occasionally guilty of that. But not at the price, one hopes, of distorting the truth. Nothing is more threatening to the integrity of the historian than to allow facts to play him or her false for the sake of a thesis. Yet this is the trap Todorov succumbs to through his unempirical approach to the Holocaust. "To know, and to let others know," he proclaims, "is one way of remaining human" (97). But the rhetorical force of this idea so consumes his energy that he neglects the accuracy of the details that presumably lead to such knowledge.

So committed is Todorov to the notion that a bureaucratic system was responsible for the murder of the Jews rather than a collection of individuals who were enthusiastically pledged to destroying them that in one crucial but damning instance the forest blinds him to the real contribution of the separate trees. He designs a chain image to suggest the fragmentation of the killing process in Auschwitz. Each link leads impersonally to the next, beginning with Hitler, who of course makes the initial decision; followed by Reinhard Heydrich, "who never sees a single suffering face"; next comes the policeman, "who merely carries out a routine order to arrest and expedite" (but never, presumably, to tear Jewish babies in two); then we have the turn of Adolf Eichmann, whose "purely technical job" is to see that the trains leave and arrive on time; after him is Rudolf Höss, the commandant, who oversees the emptying of the trains and the transfer to the gas chambers; and finally, Todorov concludes, "the last link: a group of inmates, a specialized commando that pushes the victims into the gas chambers and releases the lethal gas [*et verse dedans le gaz mortel*]." Before we have recovered from this breathtaking and infamous error, the author feels obliged to add to our knowledge: "The members of this commando are the only people who kill with their own hands." And now that we have been enlightened with the information that the only people *literally* involved in the murder of Jews in the gas chambers of Auschwitz were Jews themselves, we are relieved to learn that "they quite obviously are victims themselves, not executioners" (153).

Now how was this mistake possible, and what lies behind it? Certainly no malice, overt or covert: Todorov's tone is compassionate throughout. But the most elementary student of the Holocaust knows how Zyklon B was introduced into the gas chambers; how could Todorov have been guilty of such a lapse? If his aim had been to *represent* atrocity during the era of the Third Reich, he would have been more scrupulous in his research. But his intent from the beginning has been to *universalize* the event we call the Holocaust, implicating all of humanity as potential participants in genocide. There is a bizarre logic to his blunder that highlights the danger of any effort to schematize mass murder; it fits in with his earlier admission that "what interests me are the banal sources of exceptional actions, the ordinary attitudes that could make 'monsters' of us, too, were we to have to work in a concentration camp" (140). Primo Levi felt that such issues were irrelevant; we were victims, he said, and the Germans killed us. The rest was distracting speculation. History is not written about what other men and women might have done but did not.

One of the guilty parties in this confusion about truth is language itself. As long as we regard the Holocaust as an "exceptional action" instead of naming its specific inhuman content, we face the danger of losing contact with its reality. Todorov does not traffic in atrocities but is devoted to the ideal of "the common membership of all in the human community." This in turn leads to a reverse principle, which he offers with equally fervent conviction: "the fear one can feel in discovering that evildoers are not radically different from oneself" (225, 279). If by evildoers we mean the Germans and their collaborators who tore babies in half, buried (or burned) human beings alive, or, as in the case of the Mauthausen doctor, "operated" them to death, then we may be excused for believing that in some dimension they *are* radically different from oneself, though this need not be a statement about personal virtue *or* an explanation of a kind of behavior we may never understand. Indeed, the humble admission that we may never understand the conduct of the people we hide behind the name of perpetrators could turn out to be the most exasperating legacy of all from the multitude of crimes clustered under an abstract rubric like genocide.

Exasperation, of course, is not a very fruitful legacy, and perhaps this is why in the end Todorov chooses to distinguish between literal and exemplary memory. Having exhausted the historical roles of the functionalists and intentionalists, we may now turn to their successors, the literalists and the exemplarists. For Todorov, literal memory of the atrocities of the Holocaust, narratives of the unique painful ordeal of individual survivors, spreads "the consequences of the initial trauma over all the moments of existence." The results may be "true," but they are not very useful, in the sense that they create no new unity, no avenues for pursuing the future with fresh vigor and hope. Thus, Todorov confesses, literal memory is a "potentially risky endeavor" (258).

But there is another way of approaching the "recovered event," as Todorov calls it, and that is paradigmatically, through exemplary rather than literal memory, and this, he insists, is "truly liberating."

Since it is a view of the Holocaust shared by my artist and cleric, too, it is worth dwelling on for a moment. Why literal memory is a potentially risky endeavor Todorov does not say, but presumably he means that it may lead us into a dark cave of disenchantment from whose shadows we may never entirely escape. This is not a cheerful prospect—but neither was the murder of European Jewry. He is much more explicit, however, about the value of exemplary memory, which goes by the name of justice and involves "generalizing from the particular and applying abstract principles to concrete offenses." Anyone reading his book will see how easily this definition allows him to gloss over the concrete offenses for the sake of a higher principle. The exemplarists can only tolerate the Holocaust if it can be used as "an instrument that informs our capacity to analyze the present. . . . Only then can we tell ourselves that, at least from the viewpoint of humanity, the horrible experience of the camps will not have been in vain, that it contains lessons for us, who think we live in a completely different world" (258, 259).

Todorov has given me a label: in the sphere of memory, I am a literalist, not an exemplarist. I feel no impulse, not the slightest, to reclaim meaning from Holocaust atrocity or to embrace a Lincolnesque rhetoric seeking to persuade us that "the horrible experience of the camps will not have been in vain." There is nothing to be learned from a baby torn in two or a woman buried alive. But Todorov does unwittingly provide some helpful insight into the motives and strategy of my second example of preempting the Holocaust, Judy Chicago, the title of whose work *Holocaust Project: From Darkness into Light* gives us an unsubtle glimpse of the trajectory of her thought.

Chicago, too, is an exemplarist; she could not conceive of a Holocaust project subtitled "From Light into Darkness." But her antecedent agenda is quite different from Todorov's. "My interest in issues of gender certainly prefigured my interest in the Holocaust," she admits, following this with a more dubious pronounce-ment that nonetheless gives us a further clue about what led her to venture into the realms of mass murder: "Most people," she writes, "have not paid any attention to the fact that the architects of the Third Reich were *all* men."[4] Any inquiry that begins with a fixed premise and then seeks evidence to support it risks lapsing into a blinkered view of history. We shall have to see whether Chicago's belief in a link between patriarchy and mass murder, masculinity and Nazi ideology, entices us into further darkness, or greater light.

Judy Chicago's Holocaust education is enormously instructive, since she is perfectly frank about the tabula rasa of her mind as she began her investigation. It may surprise us to learn that a grown woman, an artist, was "ignorant" of the Holocaust as recently as 1985, but because she was not alone in her oblivion—millions of Americans share her unawareness—it would not be fair to charge her with anything more than a negligence of history. And her procedure for trying to remedy the defect is commendable: she watches Claude Lanzmann's *Shoah* and survivor testimonies, reads a library of standard Holocaust works (though her judgment here is sometimes questionable), and together with her photographer husband visits many sites of the disaster. Her initial response is far from trivial; indeed, to anyone who has tried to initiate students into the subject, it is both honest and familiar:

> After a while, I realized that some of my basic
> assumptions about people and the world were being
> profoundly challenged by the information I was
> encountering. I had always trusted people and believed
> the world to be a relatively fair and just place. Of course,
> I knew that terrible events happened, but I tended to see
> those as isolated phenomena. Confronting the
> Holocaust brought me face to face with a level of reality
> beyond anything I'd experienced before: millions of

people murdered, millions more enslaved, millions made to suffer, while the world turned its back on the implementation of the Final Solution. I couldn't take it all in; it was too painful, and I was a long way from understanding what it meant about human beings and the world in which we live. [8]

We seem to be encountering the incipient deconstruction of a natural idealist. At this point, two roads diverge in a yellow wood, one the potentially risky path of the literalists, the other planted by the exemplarists with what Todorov calls lessons that "can all be evaluated according to certain universal rational criteria that underlie human dialogue."[5] Judy Chicago hardly hesitates in her decision, pursuing the latter with an evolving enthusiasm that betrays her unwillingness to surrender a prior commitment to universal criteria and human dialogue.

Instead of considering the possibility of disjunction, of rupture between familiar forms of violence and the explosive savagery of the Final Solution, Chicago intuitively seizes on connections—a true exemplarist. "I began to perceive," she admits, "that the unique Jewish experience of the Holocaust could be a window into an aspect of the unarticulated but universal human experience of victimization." Now this is a perfectly admissible analytical approach, but it creates a problem to which exemplarists have found no satisfactory solution: how to express the universal human experience of victimization while honoring, in Chicago's words, "the particularity of the Holocaust as a historical event." The answer is that in this respect exemplarism is a self-defeating strategy. You *cannot* honor the particularity of the Holocaust in its uniquely Jewish features if your basic intention is to use it to illustrate the universality of suffering and evil, and make it into a bridge toward the creation of "a new global community based on shared human values." Distinctions evaporate amid the ardor of reformist zeal:

"To me," Chicago confesses rather early in her investigation, "one of the most important aspects of the Jewish experience of the Holocaust is that it provides us with a graphic demonstration of the vulnerability of all human beings and, by extension, of all species and our fragile planet as well."[6] There are those, however, who might find more than a touch of the trivial in linking the fate of the spotted owl or the ozone layer to the doom of European Jewry.

Perhaps visionaries like Todorov and Chicago who have programs for "creating a more peaceful and equitable world" should resist the temptation to include the Holocaust in their agenda—but the fashion is upon us, and no effort to co-opt mass murder for noble ends can be simply dismissed. Do we ignore, or at least distort history when we agree, as Chicago does, that the "fact of patriarchy" made the Holocaust possible? She admits frankly that feminism is the philosophical framework "that provides the underpinnings for the *Holocaust Project*," and we need now to ask where this leads and what insights into the Jewish catastrophe it supplies.

As it turns out, Chicago's education in Holocaust matters only assumes the formality of impartial historical inquiry, because her feminist beliefs color her conclusions from the beginning. There is absolutely nothing wrong with regarding "reverence for the feminine as an essential step toward the humanization of the world," but when the price we pay is a reductive misrepresentation of everything that doesn't agree with this position, then analysis becomes a matter of finding the proper file drawer and label for Holocaust discourse and commentary withers into a mere system for classification. Citing only Elie Wiesel as an example, Chicago concludes that "most Holocaust literature written by men . . . almost invariably stresses the uniqueness and mystery of the Holocaust," whereas, in the opinion of a single woman survivor whom she quotes, "focusing on the female experience of the Holocaust helps us move toward, rather than away from, an understanding of our human connectedness and helps repair the human fabric of community" (10, 11). The notion that "connectedness" in representing Holocaust experience is primarily the property of a single sex and not a dual-gendered thing ignores the familiar male bonding between Primo Levi and Alberto, Elie Wiesel and his father, Vladek Spiegelman (in *Maus*) and various camp inmates, Viktor Frankl and his barrack-mates when he restores their flagging spirits with an all-night reassuring harangue. I am speaking not of a dispute between patriarchy and feminism but of the need to multiply the voices we hear, and to go on multiplying them, before we conjure up gender differences that will withstand authoritative scrutiny. And this Judy Chicago has not done.

The aesthetic stance of the *Holocaust Project* also requires appraisal, because it reflects a problem that Chicago shares with many others who enter the realm of Holocaust darkness in pursuit of light. Responding to a reading of Jerzy Kosinski's *The Painted Bird,* she writes, "Being so graphic scares me, as it has to do with letting go on a level beyond what I've ever done before. Moreover, I'm afraid that what I'll create will be ugly." Mass murder is never pretty, so this would not be a problem for an artist willing to be guided by her material instead of needing to examine it selectively for data to verify her thematic concerns. As part of her scholarly investigation, Chicago also reads Yitzhak Arad's study of *The Operation Reinhard Death Camps* but can only manage forty-five minutes a day. Then she takes a furlough: "I've stopped reading for a while; that book on the Nazi killing operation at the extermination camps really depressed me" (26, 89). This retreat is characteristic of the exemplarist position, and we encounter it again and again; apparently, woman's search for meaning in the Holocaust, like man's, must surmount the merely depressing if it is to transcend the literal horrors and leave us with a more consoling vision.

Chicago's demurral is an honest admission; not many can tolerate a daily diet of atrocity. But Arad's work is not about moral life in the concentration camps any more than it furnishes evidence for a rivalry between patriarchy and sisterhood in Treblinka. Its theme is the murder of Jews in mobile killing vans and gas chambers, and even the most stalwart among us might find it depressing. Nor is Chicago alone in responding by needing—not only wanting, but needing—to find a way out of its darkness back into light. Exemplarism was born of this psychological impulse to uncover in the spiritual economy of the world some reassuring lesson to neutralize the depressing fact of mass murder.

If Jewish experience in the Holocaust can be made to "stand for" something else, some "larger human experience," whether a testimony to the integrity of the moral self, as in Todorov, or, in the case of Judy Chicago, a positive statement about the human condition in general, then the intolerable might seem more tolerable through the sheer invocation of patterns or analogies. Whatever the intention, the result is to dilute or diffuse the particularity of mass murder. And indeed, the quest for connections is an essential ingredient of the *Holocaust Project,* though some might question the worth of the comparisons it leads to: "I began to wonder about the ethical distinction," Chicago writes, "between processing pigs and doing the same to people defined as pigs." A moment of reflection on how the German military cherished their horses and dogs might have forestalled this effort to establish a link between animal rights and human slaughter. But her view grows more all-encompassing as she continues: "What is the relationship, for example, between what happened to the Jews and the extermination of the Aborigines in Australia or the Native Americans?" (58, 96). The drift toward the universal is anything but accidental; its sources lie in the fear and depression that the material itself initiates.

Perhaps with a certain amount of naïveté, Chicago discovers what the creative imagination has to face when it enters the vestibule of Holocaust atrocity: "Making art about a subject as overwhelming as this one is turning out to be is going to take an exceedingly long time. But I don't want to spend too many years on such dreadful material—it takes all the joy out of life!" (62–63). This is in fact a genuine challenge to anyone crossing the frontier that separates Holocaust landscapes from ordinary space. We all find our own beacon to guide us into this eclipsed terrain. But like Todorov, Chicago seems willing to complete the journey only if she can return exalted—and able to exalt us—by the adventure. And this she resolves to do through her vision in the *Holocaust Project*.

The technique Chicago and her husband devised for presenting this vision is ingenious, and if her talent as a painter had been greater and her universalizing impulse more restrained, the effect might have been truly impressive. She knows that Holocaust art must be rooted in the veracity of the subject, so the decision to include photographs of places like Treblinka in the final panels reflects an original and potentially powerful design. But her goal is not the kind of insight into the enigmas of atrocity that art can generate; "painting," she insists, "can provide a means of transformation." Why so much Holocaust commentary must have a cause to plead or a campaign to launch is not entirely clear to me, but I suspect it has something to do with the dreadful nature of the subject. For Chicago, what begins as a Holocaust Project ends up as a philanthropic scheme: to be included, photographs may not be too horrific, and the measure becomes "what the aesthetic limits are in terms of what I can and cannot transform" (50, 135).

Art thus plays hostage to humanitarian zeal: the culminating work in the series, painted on vividly colored stained glass, is called "Rainbow Shabbat," and depicts the beginning of a Sabbath meal. At one end of the table, a Jewish woman is about to bless the candles; at the other end, a Jewish man raises the kiddush cup. The seated guests, most with an arm on a neighbor's shoulder and a smile on their faces, include a white priest, an African, an Asian, an Arab, and some children. Beneath the table, a cat and dog lie peacefully together, reminding us that animal abuse is one of the many atrocities in contemporary society for which the Holocaust is a precedent. If we have ever been uncertain about the agenda of the project, small panels containing Stars of David at either end of the tableau cement its intent; they contain Yiddish and English versions of a prayer to embrace us all: "Heal those broken souls who have no peace and lead us all from darkness into light." No one could quarrel with this sentiment, but for a context like the Holocaust, it does not begin to address the question how to heal. In my copy of Chicago's text, the Yiddish is printed upside down (it was corrected in subsequent printings), as if some mischievous spirit of contradiction afloat in the Holocaust universe wished to sabotage her plan, in her words, "to transform these images of intense human struggle into a visual atmosphere of hope and integration" (163). That life goes on after death is by now a platitude; that *death* may also go on after death seems a plight beyond the range of the exemplarist imagination.

I turn now to the last advocate for an exemplarist position, and in many ways the most difficult one to deal with—the Christian theologian Franz Jozef van Beeck. In 1992 he delivered a talk at Cornell University called "Two Kindly Jewish Men: A Sermon in Memory of the Shoa," which initiated a Jewish-Christian dialogue whose echoes will close my analysis—and, I hope, clarify some of the distinctions I have been examining. In a letter before delivering the sermon, van Beeck admitted to his friend the Jewish theologian and scholar Eugene Borowitz—one of the two men to whom he eventually dedicated his talk—"that my sermon was the first piece I have ever written on the Holocaust myself, and that I had hardly ever discussed it in depth with anybody, Jew or Gentile."[7] This does not necessarily mean that his comments are superficial, because they emerge from years of silent pondering on the subject. Yet they also spring from years of eloquent speaking on Christian issues, and the influence of that kind of discourse, the particular idiom that verbalizes its convictions, testifies to the deficiency of certain language for analyzing the Holocaust when it is imposed on the topic with little consideration for its adequacy.

Like Todorov, who confessed to being more interested in good than in evil, and Judy Chicago, who admitted that her universalist tendencies determined her approach to the Holocaust, van Beeck has a fixed initial position that colors his response to the murder of European Jewry: "I have never," he concedes, "been able to feel raw rage or indignation at the Holocaust and its atrocities; I often used to wonder why." Perhaps this attitude is a consequence of his genuinely kind nature; perhaps it is a failure of imagination. In any event, when Father van Beeck speaks of Hitler as "a little man with a shrill voice and a large ego and a murderous theory," one begins to wonder whether a failure of imagination may not indeed be part of the problem.[8] Monstrous deeds require monstrous words to conjure up if not the inhuman monsters who did not create them, then at least the inhuman human beings who did. A commitment to personal restraint and decency, however admirable, is a powerful antidote to both.

There is an imagery that dramatizes the assault of mass murder on the integrity of the individual self, and one that universalizes the impact of that assault and transforms it into what Father van Beeck calls "the fellowship of the suffering and the long suffering." Maybe a sermon is an inappropriate form of discourse for approaching the Holocaust, since its style seems consciously tailored to minimize atrocity. Is it either consoling *or* illuminating to hear that we live in a world "where goodness and virtue will never quite succeed in being victorious"? Is it unfair to inquire whether we have moved one inch beyond Job when we are told that we also live in a world "in which unjust suffering borne in patience is not infrequently a sign of intimacy with God"? Radical division is simply impermissible to the kind of thinking that, as this particular form of Christian discourse does, wants to see spring from the ruins of the Holocaust "hope for a humanity renewed by kindness" (178, 182).

Different imagery, however, leads in different directions. Through an odd coincidence, the other person to whom Father van Beeck dedicates his sermon is named Paul Davidowits, a Holocaust survivor whose story I happen to know well because I have written about it in *Holocaust Testimonies*. Paul D.—the name under which his testimony is classified—tells of a Greek Orthodox priest in his native Slovakia who agreed to supply false certificates verifying that certain Jewish families had converted to Christianity before 1938 (thus exempting them temporarily from deportation), provided parents were willing to have any children in the family baptized into the Greek Orthodox faith. Paul D.'s parents agreed to his baptism and received the false certificates.

This part of his narrative rouses in Paul D. the memory of a dream or vision he had shortly afterward, which he recalls in vivid detail: "I'm on a meadow, and there are Jewish kids playing around me. And at one point they move away from me, and I am alone on this meadow. And God appears before me. And he's a mountain. And God holds in his hands an axe. And he just goes [raising his hands], takes the axe over his head, and with a full swing splits me in half. And I just break [gesturing] into two." At this juncture the interviewer, obviously an exemplarist in training, inquires, "Jew and Christian?" to which Paul, a confirmed literalist, replies: "I think it's more like killing me. Like punishment. It doesn't feel like Jew and Christian. It feels like annihilation." Then he adds, "I tried to be Christian, but it didn't work."[9]

Paul D.'s parable of a cosmic rift that throbs with division rather than union or communion reflects a further split within his self. Filtered through his awareness of future events, his dream foretells the fate of the Jewish children playing nearby (for whom being a Jew didn't help any more than trying to be a Christian did), as well as of his own shattered identity in its futile task of finding a "self" that might help him to survive. His memory of his dilemma during those critical years accents killing and annihilation, not reconciliation—in himself, with his fellow Jews, or the God of Jews and of Christians.

It is a bitter bequest from a threatened life, and it sits uneasily on the consciousness as we return to Father van Beeck's plea to his Jewish brothers to close "the cosmic gap between the death-camp operators and their Jewish and other victims." Does Eugene Borowitz point to an imperishable breach between attitudes, two ways of approaching the legacy of the Holocaust, when he insists that he can not speak "of compassion and mercy without an equal emphasis on the imperative of pursuing justice"? Justice here is more than an abstract concept, because it invokes crimes in the past that will not tolerate amnesia. Compassion and mercy, by contrast, summon us into a future harmony, what van Beeck envisions as "the actual embracing of all human persons, even if we have to overcome deep, deep revulsion to do so."[10] His position is not that different from Tzvetan Todorov's or Judy Chicago's: all three seek an affinity between what van Beeck calls "humanity acquired by enduring human cruelty and humanity acquired by experiencing human compassion."[11]

Nowhere is the poverty of words more evident than in the attempt to portray the deeds of the Germans and their collaborators through expressions like "deep revulsion" and "human cruelty." The impulse toward universalization here infiltrates vocabulary itself, and the best way to puncture its pretensions is by juxtaposing it with an episode of atrocity and asking ourselves what "enduring human cruelty," can possibly mean, for the victims or ourselves, in its presence. Near the end of his exhaustive re-creation of his ancestral village in Poland, the shtetl of Konin, Theo Richmond uncovers some testimony that describes the fate of the Jews of that town and its vicinity. It is in a protocol taken by the Soviets a few months after war's end from an eyewitness to the slaughter, a Polish Catholic and member of the underground who was forced by the Gestapo to gather the clothing and belongings of the victims. I am convinced that any analysis of a promising moral and spiritual condition, both in the camps and in post-Holocaust society, remains flawed unless it works *through* and not around the details of such moments as these, refusing to preempt them for the sake of a larger ideal. They may leave us aghast, but they support the belief that voyagers to the haven of exemplary behavior risk running aground unless they set sail in the vessels of Holocaust atrocity.

The witness, who after his gruesome task in the woods of Kazimierz Biskupi, was sent to Mauthausen and its subcamp at Gusen, describes two pits in a clearing, the larger one covered on its bottom by a layer of quicklime. Then he continues:

> [The Gestapo] ordered the assembled Jews to strip—first those who were standing near the large pit. Then they ordered the naked people to go down into both pits and jump into the larger pit. I could not describe the wailing and the crying. Some Jews were jumping without an order—even most of them—some were resisting and they were being beaten about and pushed down. Some mothers jumped in holding their children, some were throwing their children in, others were flinging their children aside. Still others threw the children in first and then jumped in. . . . This lasted until noon and then a lorry came from the road and stopped on the path by the clearing. I noticed four vat-like containers. Then the Germans set up a small motor—it was probably a pump— connected it with hoses to one of the vats and two of them brought the hoses from the motor up to the pit. They started the motor and the two Gestapo men began to pour some liquid, like water, on the Jews. But I am not

sure what the liquid was. While pumping, they were connecting hoses to the other containers, one by one. Apparently, because of the slaking of the lime, people in the pit were boiling alive. The cries were so terrible that we who were sitting by the piles of clothing began to tear pieces of stuff to stop our ears. The crying of those boiling in the pit was joined by the wailing and lamentation of the Jews waiting for their perdition. All this lasted perhaps two hours, perhaps longer.[12]

Nothing we hear from well-intentioned commentators like Tzvetan Todorov about moral life in the concentration camps, or from Judy Chicago about the light of human community emerging from Holocaust darkness, or from Franz Josef van Beeck about the "fellowship of the suffering and the long suffering" or closing "the cosmic gap between the death-camp operators and their Jewish and other victims" can silence the cries of those hundreds of Jews being boiled to death in an acid bath. There is simply no connection between our ordinary suffering and their unprecedented agony, nor do our trivial inclinations toward sin resemble in any way the minds that devised such terminal torture. Literalist discourse about the Holocaust—and I must stress that I am speaking *only* about the Holocaust—leads nowhere but back into the pit of destruction. At least it has the grace to acknowledge that we learn nothing from the misery it finds there.

Legacy in Gray

The Ordeal of Primo Levi

In measuring the enormous achievements of Primo Levi, I am struck first of all by the way American publishers have tried to twist his intentions as a writer into an affirmative direction by altering the titles of his books. His first and most famous work, *If This Is a Man,* appeared as *Survival in Auschwitz: The Nazi Assault on Humanity,* changing a hesitant inquiry into a confident manifesto, even though Levi to the end of his life continued to explore the morally uncertain meaning of the experience we call "survival." Its sequel, *The Truce,* appeared as *The Reawakening,* again giving a positive spin to a decidedly neutral term, since an armistice between Auschwitz and the future can hardly be considered a revival from the realm of permanent sleep. And the anecdotal volume about Auschwitz published in Italy simply as *Lilith and Other Tales* is changed in the United States into *Moments of Reprieve.* Such revised titles might easily deceive readers into believing that Levi's main interest was to mine gleaming nuggets of human fellowship from the barren landscape of Auschwitz.

It was not. In a series of interviews conducted during the closing years of his life, Levi described precisely the varied population he found upon arrival in the camp: "This was the human material

I had around me. Among these unfortunates, there was no solidarity, none at all, and this lack was the first and biggest trauma. I
and the others who'd been transported with me had thought, na-
ively, 'However bad it may be, we'll find comrades.' It didn't turn
out that way. We found enemies, not comrades."[1] Of course, Levi
was not pleased to reach this conclusion. He remembered his close
friend Alberto in Auschwitz, who shared equally whatever scarce
provisions he could find, or the "free" Italian bricklayer Lorenzo,
who every day for many months sneaked Levi a large extra portion
of soup. But he also recalled that the general spirit of Auschwitz
reflected rivalry rather than unity. And he never ceased to be troubled by this memory of strife.

Throughout his writings on Auschwitz, Levi conducted an
ongoing but ultimately futile quest to find a bond linking physical
and moral survival. He believed in the value of community, while
confessing that staying alive in the camp required the privileged to
oppress the unprivileged. He strove to remain decent while admitting that survival "without renunciation of any part of one's own
moral world" was conceded only to martyrs and saints, not the
majority of inmates—presumably including himself.[2] He was too
honest to insist that survival was a tale of spiritual triumph. The
camp experience sabotaged the ethical vision that he cherished as a
human being. Unwilling to abandon that vision, he tried in vain to
restore a moral balance to the post-Auschwitz universe in which he
lived. But like so many other survivors, he had to admit the dismal
truth that the world had learned virtually nothing from the mass
murder of European Jewry. Until his death, he wavered between
the same hope and despair about the human condition that had
assailed him during his year in the camp. He left us with a legacy
neither radiant nor grim, only gray, dimmed by the similar doubts
that still hang over the last moments of his life.

One of Levi's major tasks as a writer was to remind his readers,
as he quaintly put it, that "Auschwitz etiquette was different from

ours."[3] He tells amusingly of how he "corrupted" an innocent new Hungarian arrival who at first believed that work in Auschwitz must be carried out with the same discipline and rigor as work anywhere else. Levi resolves to "convert" his disciple by undermining the integrity that is sure to doom him: "I tried to convince him of a few recent discoveries of mine (in truth, not yet well digested): that down there, in order to get by, it was necessary to get busy, to organize illegal food, dodge work, find influential friends, hide one's thoughts, steal, and lie; that whoever did not do so was soon dead, and that his saintliness seemed dangerous to me and out of place."[4] These are among the commandments inscribed on the Tables of the Law in Auschwitz, and we still flinch at the image of honorable men and women being forced to endorse them in order to stay alive. Levi's disciple soon absorbs the wisdom of learning to steal.

Did this represent a temporary adjustment in values required by an abnormally oppressive situation or a permanent inroad on integrity that would leave its scars long after war's end? Levi wrestled all his life with this question. Unlike Viktor Frankl, he avoided heroizing himself by finding formulas for spiritual vigor to let him rise above his lapsing fellow prisoners. He never insisted on unique personal strengths that distanced him from others. He offered instead a group portrait of diminished human beings who were compromised by their special knowledge:

> There was little feeling of *camaraderie* among us. It was
> confined to compatriots, and even toward them it was
> weakened by the minimal life conditions. It was actually
> zero, indeed negative, with regard to newcomers. In this
> and many other respects we had greatly retrogressed and
> become hardened. And in the "new" fellow prisoner we
> tended to see an alien, an oafish, cumbersome barbarian
> who took up space and time, and bread, who did not
> know the unspoken but ironclad rules of coexistence and

survival, and who, moreover, complained (and for the wrong reasons) in an irritating and ridiculous manner because just a few days back he was still at home, or at least outside the barbed wire.[5]

These are not the words of a man still seething with the recent memories of his painful encounter with moral disorder but the feelings of a writer more than thirty years after the event. For Levi, the memory of atrocity never faded, nor did it dwindle into a sentimental tale of communal resistance against a ruthless foe. He stifled all temptations to allow the haze of time to obscure his initial view that the offense of Auschwitz was an "inexhaustible fount of evil."[6]

One of the greatest values of Primo Levi's work is that it permits us to measure the impact of chronology, both temporal and moral, on the original deeds of atrocity. Because he returned again and again to the ordeal of Auschwitz, Levi could pursue the truths of the camp down the twisting corridors of history as well as into the dark recesses of his own inner life. To be sure, freedom followed imprisonment, for those lucky enough to survive, just as efforts at justice followed the hideous crime. But Levi quickly learned that they were not enough to decontaminate or redeem the evil spewed forth by Nazi Germany. In the opening pages of *The Truce* he had described how the moment of liberation had filled the souls of survivors with joy, but also with a painful sense of shame, "so that we should have liked to wash our consciences and our memories clean from the foulness that lay upon them; and also with anguish, because we felt that this should never happen, that now nothing could ever happen good and pure enough to rub out our past, and that the scars of the outrage would remain within us forever, and in the memories of those who saw it, and in the places where it occurred, and in the stories we should tell of it" (12–13). Although *The Truce* is Levi's account of the long journey back from the camp to his place of birth, he ends it not with a celebration of reunion but with a report of a "dream full of horror" that continued to visit him after his deliverance. For me, it persists as the most frightening image in any of his works. In that dream, he writes, sitting among family or friends in a peaceful environment,

> I feel a deep and subtle anguish, the definite sensation of an impending threat. And in fact, as the dream proceeds, slowly or brutally, each time in a different way, everything collapses and disintegrates around me, the scenery, the walls, the people, while the anguish becomes more intense and more precise. Now everything has changed to chaos; I am alone in the centre of a grey and turbid nothing, and now, I *know* what this thing means, and I also know that I have always known it; I am in the Lager [the camp] once more, and nothing is true outside the Lager. All the rest was a brief pause, a deception of the senses, a dream; my family, nature in flower, my home. [222]

Levi was not the only survivor haunted by this kind of recurrent dream. Its dark verdict that "nothing is true outside the Lager" was in constant conflict with the post-Auschwitz hopes of humanity and society, a conflict Levi returned to throughout his career.

If nothing is true outside the Lager, we need to explore Levi's version of what was true *inside* it, and the text of his first book, *If This Is a Man* (or *Survival in Auschwitz*) provides ample material for such an investigation. There, he developed a doctrine of multiple possibilities to clarify the varied responses to the threats that Auschwitz imposed on the self struggling to stay alive. Readers seeking simple explanations pounce on isolated lines or episodes as if they were hidden keys to the mystery of why one Jew survived while another did not. But Levi's strategy duplicates the experience of a novice entering an unfamiliar milieu whose rules he has not yet understood. He offers us the "lessons" as he learns them himself; part of our education is to discern that what we master one day we may have to abandon the next, since no successful gesture can be separated from others that may subvert them.

One of the first rules Levi digests is not to ask why something is so. Reason does not reign in Auschwitz. Yet if one cannot fathom the rituals that replace it, one is doomed. Suffering from thirst soon after his arrival, Levi reaches out of a barrack window and breaks off an icicle; a prowling guard brutally snatches it away from him. "Warum?" (Why?) Levi innocently asks with his limited German, and the guard's reply—"Hier ist kein warum" (There is no why here)—exposes the basic nature of the place: questions have no answers, so it is useless to ask any. There are ways of behaving that hasten death, and other ways that postpone it: between these narrow margins lay the zone where the prisoner in Auschwitz was able to maneuver.

Today we take for granted the role of a common language in helping us to express needs, form bonds, and define the moral borders of the universe we live in. But Levi discovered in Auschwitz what he called "a perpetual Babel, in which everyone shouts orders and threats in languages never heard before, and woe betide whoever fails to grasp the meaning."[7] He invites us to share this confusion of tongues by threading through his text foreign words, phrases, and sentences that pile up until they form a new global lexicon of Holocaust discourse. Only by feeling some ease with such discourse can readers, together with Levi, find their way amid this confusion of tongues. Levi understood that we could not share the physical distress of the new arrival, who quickly learns that "the Lager is hunger: we ourselves are hunger, living hunger" (74). He realized that his audience would have trouble embracing this cramped view of the self. So he offered entry into the world of Auschwitz by extending his doctrine of multiple possibilities from human behavior to the words that described it.

Readers of *If This Is a Man* may wish that they had brought to the encounter an armful of dictionaries. The polyglot vocabulary is exasperating: *Lager. Häftling. Blockälteste. Muselmann. Klepsi, klepsi. Menaschka. Wäschetauschen. Wstawach. Wer hat noch zu fressen? La propreté, c'est la santé.* Without an interpreter, what average reader can make his or her way through such a colloquial maze? Either you adapt to the peculiar idiom of this multilingual domain, or you falter—and soon, you die. What better way to confront the reader with the potentially fatal verbal challenge that Levi and his comrades faced every day? In a few places, he accentuates this Babel of tongues by giving the options for a single word: "bread-Brot-Broid-chleb-pain-lechem-keynér," initiating us into his macrocosm not only in Italian but also in English, German, Yiddish, Polish and Russian, French, Hebrew, and Hungarian (39).

Levi is not playing linguistic games but stressing the importance of translating Auschwitz into terms unfamiliar to our native ear. If naming stabilizes reality, continual renaming unsettles it, and the deeper meaning of Levi's Babel of tongues is that not only verbal but also moral values mutate in this volatile realm. Outside Auschwitz, what sense can we assign to the decree that "death begins with the shoes," or to the reminder that "everything can be stolen, in fact is automatically stolen as soon as attention is relaxed" (34, 33)? Like a voracious beast, camp routines consume prized laws of conduct, leaving an ethical void into which seep cynical maxims like the ones Levi lists. The prisoner who could not adapt to such unorthodox principles—Levi himself said they inspired stories for a new Bible—speedily perished. And the reader who cannot adjust to the impact of such a system on otherwise decent men and women will never cross the frontier into their world—one that eroded their spiritual stamina and reduced them to primitive means for staying alive, unseemly, at least in our eyes, for civilized human beings.

But Levi is not interested in judging, and he discourages us from doing so. His chief goal is to report the way it was, an existence full of uncertainty and contradictions. He manages to furnish us simultaneously with a chronological and durational narrative, the one beginning with arrest and deportation and ending at the point of liberation, and the other full of harsh moments and episodes that will remain engraved in memory, untouched by the passage of time. In the central narrative of *If This Is a Man,* the inmate in Auschwitz lives from hour to hour, meal to meal, evening to dawn, the normal rhythms of temporal existence having been upset by the demands of keeping the body intact through one more roll call. Only after the Germans flee the approaching Russians, leaving Levi and a few hundred other ill prisoners behind, does the text return to the daily flow of time: suddenly, Levi begins to date his entries.

With the future restored, the reader breathes a sigh of relief, though Philip Roth has described the interval between German departure and Russian arrival as a version of Robinson Crusoe in Hell. Weakened by illness, Levi and a comrade nonetheless leave the crude infirmary where they and other starving patients are recovering from scarlet fever to scavenge the landscape for provisions: turnips, frozen potatoes, whatever is edible. Later they seek a source of heat and build a makeshift stove. But their human quest is framed by an event that casts lurid shadows over their efforts: as the Germans leave, an air raid strikes the camp. Levi's description confirms the aptness of Roth's portrayal: "Two huts were burning fiercely, another two had been pulverized, but they were all empty. Dozens of patients arrived, naked and wretched, from a hut threatened by fire: they asked for shelter. It was impossible to take them in. They insisted, begging and threatening in many languages. We had to barricade the door. They dragged themselves elsewhere, lit up by the flames, barefoot in the melting snow" (157). If we did not know that we were facing victims rather than sinners, we might mistake this for a setting from Dante's *Inferno.* Despite the return of chronological time and the promise of liberation, the spirit of Babel prevails. Auschwitz still prohibits the shift to universal fellowship, because on the brink of freedom those stricken by scarlet fever fear further contagion from those infected with typhus or diphtheria.

As Levi records in his calendar the march toward rescue, he cannot avoid entries which impede that progress, as if moments of duration threaten forever to taint the restoration of chronology to the lives of those lucky enough to survive. In the ward adjoining Levi's hut lie wretches suffering from dysentery; their cries can be heard through the thin wall:

> Naturally I would have liked to have helped them, given the means and the strength, if for no other reason than to stop their crying. In the evening when all the work was finished, conquering my tiredness and disgust, I dragged myself gropingly along the dark, filthy corridor to their ward with a bowl of water and the remainder of our day's soup. The result was that from then on, through the thin wall, the whole diarrhea ward shouted my name day and night with the accents of all the languages of Europe, accompanied by the incomprehensible prayers, without my being able to do anything about it. I felt like crying, I could have cursed them. [166]

The principle of selective caring that allowed a few to help each other while the rest were left to die was a flawed compromise bequeathed by the evil of Auschwitz. Even after the Germans have fled, Levi is left with the sorrowful paradox that each advance is accompanied by a simultaneous retreat.

No section in the text of *If This Is a Man* stresses that legacy more than the one immediately preceding the narrative's return to a chronological rhythm. The last episode Levi records before he begins to date his entries highlights the crucial role of durational time in the memory of those who outlived the ordeal. The chapter itself is called "The Last One," and it refers to the final cry of the doomed man whose hanging Levi and his friend Alberto are about to witness: "Kameraden, ich bin der Letzte!" (Comrades, I am the last one!). The victim was one of the group who wrecked a crematorium abutting the gas chambers in October 1944. But instead of being heartened by this futile deed of heroism, Levi and Alberto are only reminded of their own inertia and submissiveness: like everyone else required to watch the execution, they stand silently, "bent and gray, our heads dropped" (149).

The juxtaposition of the closing chapters of Levi's account of Auschwitz, "The Last One" and "The Story of Ten Days," forces us to consider the twin temporal possibilities for reading the text and for reflecting on its contents. Passage of time and fixation in time, movement toward release and memory anchored in scenes like the hanging tug at our responses, seeking affinity where perhaps none exists. But one thing is sure: durational moments send their roots into unexplored depths of the self, where they continue to feed in ways that even Levi may never have completely understood.

This does not mean, however, that he was unaware of the crisis. Being a helpless spectator to the murder of others will remain for him a constant reminder of personal defeat, a source of shame that nothing can erase. Nowhere is the meaning of his title, *If This Is a Man,* more clearly invoked than in the lines he wrote following the report of the hanging: "To destroy a man is difficult, almost as difficult as to create one: it has not been easy, nor quick, but you Germans have succeeded. Here we are, docile under your gaze; from our side you have nothing more to fear; no acts of violence, no words of defiance, not even a look of judgment" (150). In Levi's ongoing saga of Auschwitz, this joint paralysis of the physical and moral will both is and is not the sign of a final state of being. Chronological time allowed Levi, through the chance of survival, to free himself from this paralysis and to rejoin the human community as a productive chemist and a successful writer. But durational time plunged him back into the chaos of his Auschwitz past, where even forty years after the event he was still exploring the meaning of shame and judgment, and that gray zone where man's vaunted moral self had lost its dignity and never found a way to reclaim it.

As I said at the outset, Levi could never equate the accident of survival with any form of triumph. In the next-to-last entry of his closing calendar in *If This Is a Man,* the day before the Russians arrive, Levi wrote: "It is man who kills, man who creates or suffers injustice: it is no longer man who, having lost all restraint, shares his bed with a corpse. Whoever waits for his neighbor to die in order to take his piece of bread is, albeit guiltless, further from the model of thinking man than the most primitive pigmy or the most vicious sadist" (171–172). These are among the bleakest words that Levi ever wrote, but they should not be mistaken for an expression of reproach, either of Levi himself or of others. As a witness to the demeaning atmosphere that surrounded him, he was too honest to alter it for the sake of a posterity that needed to salvage some message of hope from this quagmire of despair. But he was wary about one crucial issue: though the victims may seem crushed by their misfortune, the fault lay not with them but with "you Germans," the agents of the evil that consumed their moral strength and, for most, their physical lives.

Four decades later, perhaps realizing how some of the gloomiest moments in *If This Is a Man* might be misread as an effort to blame the victims, Levi returned in *The Drowned and the Saved* to this troublesome theme. One popular gambit in the postwar years to "explain" the atrocity of the Holocaust had been the universalizing argument that what the Germans did only reflected a capacity for violence and evil buried in human nature everywhere. Levi was appalled and offended by this evasion. "I am not an expert on the unconscious and the mind's depths," he wrote, but I do know that few people are experts in this sphere and that these few are the most cautious. I do not know, and it does not much interest me to know, whether in my depths there lurks a murderer, but I do know that I was a guiltless victim and I was not a murderer. I know that the murderers existed not only in Germany, and still exist, retired or on active duty, and that to confuse them with their victims is a moral disease or an aesthetic affectation or a sinister sign of complicity; above all, it is a precious service rendered (intentionally or not) to the negators of truth.[8]

As the years passed and he noted an increasing interest in the conduct of the victims and a growing indifference to the behavior of the killers (to say nothing of the will to identify and prosecute them), Levi found himself both vexed and alarmed by the mist of misconceptions into which the outrages that had scarred his life were drifting. Among the many motives that drove him to write *The Drowned and the Saved* forty years after the collapse of Auschwitz, this must have been a leading one.

Victims in the camp could be forgiven, as Levi put it, for "drowning one by one in the stormy sea of not-understanding," because the "Lager jargon" was alien to their native vocabulary (96). But when he discovered that many of his contemporaries, and particularly the Germans themselves, were floating cheerfully in that same sea of incomprehension, he vowed to do something about it. "The further events fade into the past," he conceded in his last volume, "the more the construction of convenient truth grows and is perfected" (27). He launched a campaign against such "truths," and now that he was both a survivor of the camps and a student of their history, he had gained a perspective that allowed him to write with broader authority than had been available to him in *If This Is a Man,* which he finished during the year following his liberation. If in the beginning his role was to bear witness, in the end it included the need to weigh issues like cruelty, responsibility, and judgment. He divided his text between defending his fellow survivors from unjust charges growing out of stereotyped notions of their ordeal, and defining the criminality of the killers and their supporters in a language that leaves the nature of their crimes unmistakable.

First he had to explode the myth, still clung to by some Holocaust commentators, that suffering in Auschwitz was somehow ennobling. "It is naive, absurd, and historically false," he insisted, "to believe that an infernal system such as National Socialism sanctifies its victims: on the contrary, it degrades them, it makes them resemble itself." The shrewd inmate quickly recognized the value of associating with those in power, not in order to mimic their brutality, but so as to gain access to extra rations, for as Levi asserts, without additional sources of food, a starving and weakened prisoner lasted only two or three months in a place like Auschwitz. Some form of privilege—"large or small . . . licit or illicit"—was necessary to stay alive (40, 41). That is why Levi always argued that the only ones to feel the full horrors of Auschwitz were those who did not return.

Levi dismisses what he charitably calls "a certain hagiographic and rhetorical stylization" that credits survival to a blend of will, resistance, and inner discipline. He replaces this romantic view with a more sober and practical principle: "the harsher the oppression, the more widespread among the oppressed is the willingness to collaborate." But he would reject any effort to identify such camp behavior with the collaboration of free men and women in the Vichy or Quisling regimes in France and Norway. Just as terms like "hunger" and "thirst" were defined differently inside and outside the Lager, so a word like "collaborate," according to Levi, should be stripped of much of the scorn that clings to it in the world beyond the barbed wire: "Before discussing separately the motives that impelled some prisoners to collaborate to some extent with the Lager authorities, however, it is necessary to declare the imprudence of issuing hasty moral judgment on such human cases. Certainly, the greatest responsibility lies with the system, the very structure of the totalitarian state; the concurrent guilt on the part of individual big and small collaborators (never likable, never transparent!) is always difficult to evaluate" (43–44). Levi did not enjoy using a word like "guilt" when raising this problematic topic—and we need scarcely remind ourselves that with rare exceptions he was speaking about the lot of the Jews in all these remarks—because once again the "free" and "imprisoned" definitions did not mesh. In the end, he preferred to speak of "shame" as the primary legacy of the moral swamp into which German coercion had sunk its prey.

When Levi said that the greatest responsibility lay with the system, he set himself the task of explaining what he meant. Even as he used the term, he realized how unsatisfactory it was. On one hand, the Final Solution was a planned aggression against the Jews of Europe. Mass murder did not erupt spontaneously from the soil of Germany and the countries it occupied. On the other, Levi knew that the atrocities he witnessed and endured in Auschwitz did not follow some carefully designed plan issued by the authorities in Berlin. What the Jews suffered during deportation and in the camps was so unpredictable and *un*systematic, so dissimilar to other historical episodes of violence, that Levi felt driven to define the special quality of this event. He knew it was a complex challenge: "Thinking back with the wisdom of hindsight to those years that devastated Europe and, in the end, Germany itself, one feels torn between two opinions: Were we witnessing the rational development of an inhuman plan or a manifestation (unique in history and still unsatisfactorily explained) of collective madness? Logic intent on evil or the absence of logic? As so often happens in human affairs, the two alternatives coexisted" (106). His notion of multiple possibilities could thus be extended to Nazi Germany itself, and the killers it employed.

The idea that Levi wanted to engrave on the minds of his readers was what he called "the practice of useless cruelty." This was the prototypical, primordial German crime during the era of the Third Reich. Even some "use" can be found in the violence of war, brutal as its tactics may be: the defeat of Hitler is a prime example. The goal of useless cruelty, however, is a "desire for the suffering of others" not in order to achieve some essential military or political aim but simply for its own sake. This was an axiom of German conduct toward its enemies, particularly the Jews, and it left its victims helpless to prepare a useful response. Levi lists a few public examples, some of them well known: the executions in the Ardeatine Caves outside of Rome, and the destruction of the villages of Oradour in France and Lidice in Czechoslovakia, together with the murder of most of their inhabitants. These are cases, he says, where "the limits of reprisal, already intrinsically inhuman, were enormously surpassed" (107). Victims were so vulnerable for the very reason that they were unable to imagine a system tolerating a practice of useless cruelty that allowed the inhuman to have no limits.

The slow dying from starvation or untreated disease that was the rule in the camps for those not selected for gassing was for Levi a classic instance of the "deliberate creation of pain that was an end in itself" (109). What, he asks, was served by the combination of "gratuitous viciousness" with indifference and negligence that caused so much human misery? If swift and merciless death were the goal, one could perhaps "understand" (without condoning) such behavior. But "the useless cruelty of violated modesty," the public humiliation, especially of women, seemed an assault on dignity without purpose: "I do not believe that this transformation was ever planned or formulated in so many words at any level of the Nazi hierarchy, in any document, at any 'labor meeting.' It was a logical consequence of the system: an inhuman regime spreads and extends its inhumanity in all directions, also and especially downward; unless it meets with resistance and exceptionally strong characters, it corrupts its victims and its opponents as well" (III, 112). This returns us to the ultimate dilemma that even Primo Levi could not solve: a system may be blamed, but cannot be indicted or tried, for the practice of useless cruelty. Only its agents can, but they are concealed by that very system behind cloaks of anonymity, and in Levi's text, they do not emerge. He does not study the Bogers and Kaduks of Birkenau, the individual torturers and murderers who cheerfully embraced their regime's notion of useless cruelty and devised their own private versions of how it should be applied.

Perhaps we will never comprehend how and why such decisions were made, but every time Primo Levi mentions the subject, he returns to the site of his own internal wound. And because we have no "cure" for that wound, no satisfactory explanation, it continues to fester, in his own imagination and in ours. He tells of two ninety-year-old women in his convoy to Auschwitz who were dragged from the infirmary and loaded onto his train simply because they were Jewish. One died en route, the other was gassed on arrival. "Would it not have been simpler," Levi asks, "more 'economical,' to let them die, or perhaps kill them in their beds, instead of adding their agony to the collective agony of the transport? One is truly led to think that, in the Third Reich, the best choice, the choice imposed from above, was the one that entailed the greatest affliction, the greatest waste, the greatest physical and moral suffering" (120). But worst of all, and this is implied in everything that Levi wrote about it, is that the crime remains unpunished and unrepented. The ninety-year-old women did not drag themselves from their beds; they were taken by men who to this day are unknown, uncharged, untried, and possibly, in their *own* feelings, guiltless of any misdeeds.

The crimes were monstrous but not, as Levi maintained, the criminals. Camp guards were "obtuse brutes, not subtle demons." The violence that ran in their veins was not a moral disease but a normal and obvious expression of their roles. "I do not mean to say that they were made of a perverse human substance," Levi concedes, "different from ours (there were also sadists and psychopaths among them, but they were few)." Yet Levi, for some reason, did not seize the challenge of exploring the nature of his tormentors with the same detailed scrutiny he applied to the idiosyncrasies of his fellow prisoners. Of course, he observed them from a distance and probably did not enjoy speculating about strangers. Even though he calls the Lager his university and admits that it "taught us to look around and measure men," he chose not to measure with critical appraisal the agents of his misery, their motives or their deeds (121, 141).

Perhaps one cause is that when Levi wrote about his fellow prisoners, he wrote as a witness. Examining his tormentors would require him to advance to the level of analyst, and his natural modesty, combined with a reluctance to venture into an area where "experts" had already clouded the field, held him back. But I suspect that there is a more fundamental reason. "We are neither historians nor philosophers," he wrote in *The Drowned and the Saved,* "but witnesses, and anyway, who can say that the history of human events obeys rigorous logic, patterns. One cannot say that each turn followed from a single why: simplifications are proper only for textbooks; the whys can be many, entangled with one another or unknowable, if not actually nonexistent" (150). "Hier ist kein warum" was a lesson learned early and well, but Levi was not eager to hear that it was as valid at the end of the journey as it was at the beginning. Neither Eichmann in Jerusalem nor the accused at Nuremberg had furnished any insight into how particular individuals had assented to or participated in the crime of mass murder—merely a pastiche of excuses. It was not too difficult to tell the drowned from the saved among the victims of the camps or to decipher the reasons for the condition of each. Finding a similar distinction among the Germans, by contrast, was a daunting task, whereas further refinements were well-nigh impossible.

Levi's despondency on this subject is evident in his last book, *The Drowned and the Saved,* which closes with a chapter called "Letters from Germans," giving us a clue to what was on his mind in the final years of his foreshortened life. He identifies the "new emotion" he felt when he learned that *If This Is a Man* was to be published in Germany. Only then, in 1959, did he realize that "its true recipients, those against whom the book was aimed like a gun were they, the Germans. Now the gun was loaded." Such violent imagery is totally atypical of a man of gentle temperament like Primo Levi; it tells us how pivotal this moment must have been for him. He spoke of cornering his German readers, of settling accounts, not in order to gain revenge but to provoke a dialogue. When Levi wrote in the mid-1980s of that time in the late 1950s when he still had hoped to acquire some insight into the German mentality of the war years, he was in a good position to assess the impact of his work. *If This Is a Man* was about Auschwitz time, what I have called durational time, but Levi's German readers had seen the passage of so much chronological time that the interval had diluted rather than intensified the difference. When *If This is a Man* appeared in Germany, Levi received some sober and thoughtful letters and some eccentric and exasperating ones, too. But in a country of millions, a book read by thousands could not awaken the national self-inquiry he desired. His failure to "understand the Germans"—the useless cruelty of his travail in Auschwitz was but one example of this—lingered as a "painful void" in his life as a writer and a man (168, 174).

Although he quoted from several of the letters, Levi used the opportunity of this essay to restate his feelings about the Germans he tried to but could not understand, and he writes with a language of indictment that convinces us he could no longer divide the memory of the victimizers from the memory of the victims. He mentions the SS, of course, but "also those others, those who had believed, who not believing had kept silent, who did not have the frail courage to look into our eyes, to throw us a piece of bread, to whisper a human word." He was not interested in a spirit of reconciliation: "Almost all, but not all, had been deaf, blind, and dumb: a mass of 'invalids' surrounding a core of ferocious beasts. Almost all, though not all, had been cowardly" (169). He cited the "modest courage" of one German technician in Auschwitz who during an air raid insisted on bringing Levi and two comrades into a bunker though it was off-limits to Jews. But this only highlights the absence of courage in all the others. Levi alleged that he never hated the Germans, but he leaves no doubt that he still condemns them, and the closing words of *The Drowned and the Saved* invite his readers, especially those who rely on the ideas of others to form their response to the Holocaust, to accept such censure as a legacy that neither time nor pardon can erase:

> Let it be clear that to a greater or lesser degree all were
> responsible, but it must be just as clear that behind their
> responsibility stands that great majority of Germans who
> accepted in the beginning, out of mental laziness,
> myopic calculation, stupidity, and national pride the
> "beautiful words" of Corporal Hitler, followed him as
> long as luck and lack of scruples favored him, were swept
> away by his ruin, afflicted by deaths, misery, and
> remorse, and rehabilitated a few years later as the result
> of an unprincipled political game. [203]

These are among the sourest and most disillusioned words Primo Levi ever wrote. They betray a state of mind not usually associated with him, but that may be because he buried beneath his calm demeanor an indignation whose embers had never expired. It is reported that when Primo Levi was wheeled into the operating room for prostate surgery a few months before his death, he rolled up his sleeve and pointed to the number tattooed on his arm, saying, "That is my disease."[9]

On the book jacket of the American edition of *The Drowned and the Saved* appears an imprudent statement that reminds us how far we still have to go if we are to grasp the impact of Auschwitz on one of its most outspoken survivors: "Primo Levi's luminous writings offer a wondrous celebration of life. His universally acclaimed books remain a testament to the indomitability of the human spirit and humanity's capacity to defeat death through meaningful work, morality and art." Levi would have blanched at such mindless rhetoric, so indifferent to the complex and painful subterranean tenor of much of his work. Although he will long be remembered, he certainly did not defeat death. He left us rather with the vexing question of whether the death he eluded in Auschwitz did not finally defeat him, not as it ultimately conquers us all, but as a unique psychological wound that only graduates of Auschwitz comprehend. Readers of *If This Is a Man* know that it is as much a death story as it is a life story, and I think the same is true, though the tone may be more muted, of everything that Primo Levi ever wrote about his camp ordeal.

Gendered Suffering

Women in Holocaust Testimonies

If the world of German labor camps, concentration camps, and deathcamps has taught us anything, it is that abnormal living conditions prompt unpredictable responses. Listening to the voices of women who survived those domains reminds us of the severely diminished role that gendered behavior played during those cruel years. Even when we hear stories about mutual support among women in the camps, the context of the narratives shows us how seldom such alliances made any difference in the long-range effects of the ordeal for those who outlived it. Because it can never be segregated from the murder of the many, the survival of the few cannot be used as a measure of why some women survived and others did not.

Let me begin with the written monologue of Mado from Charlotte Delbo's trilogy *Auschwitz and After*, which appeared in full English translation only in 1995. Delbo, a non-Jew, was arrested for underground activity and sent to Auschwitz in January 1943, together with 230 other French women. Only 49 returned. Delbo visited many of them after the war, and in one of her volumes she explored the damaging effects that their interlude in the camp had on their subsequent lives. Mado, one of these survivors, reveals a neglected consequence of the camp experience, which I call the "missed destiny of dying." In our haste to celebrate renewal, we are inclined to ignore the scar that intimate contact with the death of her women friends and supporters has left on the memory and feeling of the witness.

Mado begins: "It seems to me I'm not alive. Since all are dead, it seems impossible I shouldn't be also. All dead. Mounette, Viva, Sylviane, Rosie, all the others, all the others. How could those stronger and more determined than I be dead, and I remain alive? Can one come out of there alive? No. It wasn't possible."[1] Delbo then invites us to unravel the tapestry of paradoxes that Mado weaves around the belief that she is "living without being alive"—a talking corpse. This idea recurs often enough in our encounter with the voices and faces of other women survivors to force us to admit it into our colloquy about the Holocaust. Its fate there, however, will depend on whether we let it fester or pledge to explore the sources and echoes of its taint.

Mado does not exalt her survival or the aid from her friends that helped to make it possible; instead, she mourns the death of others: "One morning, when it was still pitch dark, I woke up to the sound of roll call. Next to me, Angèle Mercier did not move. I did not shake her. Did not feel her. Without even looking at her I knew she was dead. She was the first to die next to me." Mado then gives us a lucid and honest appraisal of what it means for her to be among "those who came back": "I do what one does in life, but I know very well that this isn't life, because I know the difference between before and after." She tries to explain what she means by this: "All the efforts we made to prevent our destruction, preserve our identity, keep our former being, all these efforts could only be put to use over there [là-bas]. When we returned, this hard kernel we had forged at the core of our hearts, believing it to be solid since it had been won through boundless striving, melted, dissolved.

Nothing left. My life started over there. Before there was nothing. I no longer have what I had over there, what I had before, what I was before. Everything has been wrenched from me. What's left? Nothing. Death" (258, 259).

In other words, the immediate threats of Auschwitz led to the creation of a community among Mado and her fellow deportees that may have sustained some of them as memories of their lives before the camp faded and vanished. But that community, she says, is gone now, most of its members victims who did not return. Mado refuses to delude herself about the rupture that prevents her past from gliding into a fruitful future: "This superhuman will we summoned from our depths in order to return abandoned us as soon as we came back. Our stock was exhausted. We came back, but why? We wanted this struggle, these deaths not to have been in vain. Isn't it awful to think that Mounette died for nothing, that Viva died for nothing? Did they die that I, you, a few others might return?" (260). She knows that this question should be answered in the negative, even as she clutches at the opposite possibility in futile hope of minimal consolation.

The experience of staying alive in the camps cannot be separated from the experience of dying in the camps. The clear line that in normal times divides life from death disappeared there, and memory cannot restore it. Mado is married and has a son, but her family is unable to help her forget. It's not a matter of forgetting, she insists. You don't choose memories; memories choose you. And because of that, she cannot embrace her roles as wife and mother. Love has become a gesture, not a source of fulfillment. She can't tell this to her husband, because then he would realize that "all his caring hasn't alleviated the pain." Mado's concluding words give graphic shape to the idea that one can outlive a deathcamp without having survived it: "People believe memories grow vague, are erased by time since nothing endures against the passage of time.

That's the difference; time does not pass over me, over us. It doesn't erase anything, doesn't undo it. I'm not alive. I died in Auschwitz but no one knows it" (267).

Is Mado's story exceptional? Judging from the testimonies I have seen, some of which we will examine, I would have to conclude that numerous other women who outlived the atrocity also inhabit two worlds, the world of then and the world of now. One biological feature of their gender, the capacity to bear children, has had a singular impact on their efforts to confront their ordeal, an impact that they could not and cannot share with male inmates. The phenomenon of maternity continues to haunt them with the memory and anticipation of a special suffering that lacks any redeeming balance. When Charlotte Delbo went to visit one of her Auschwitz companions in a lying-in hospital in Paris after the war, her friend complained that her newborn infant brought her no joy; all she could think about was the children in Auschwitz being sent to their death in the gas chambers. Like Mado, this woman had not escaped the taint of memory that frustrated her bid to reclaim her role as mother.

Because this dilemma seems specific to women, let us pursue it for a moment. In her testimony, Holocaust survivor Sally H. recalls the march to the train that would carry most of her family to their death in Auschwitz. Her most vivid memory is of a young girl among the deportees who was in an advanced stage of pregnancy:

> People did get married in the ghetto. People think that
> the ghetto was just, you know, closed in—they were
> getting married, because people had hope things would
> go on. And there was that, my mother's, a friend's
> daughter. She was eighteen years old, Rachel Goldfarb. I
> have to mention names, they're not here. She got
> married, and she got pregnant, became pregnant. And
> when we had the, when they took us out of the city we

didn't have a train, there were no trains, to walk to the trains . . . I don't know the mileage to Garbatka. And I always remember Rachel, she had a very big stomach, I was eleven and a half, close to twelve. So at the time, you don't think about things like this. She was pregnant, and she was very big. It was very hot, it was the second day of Succoth, it happened to be very hot. And she was wearing a trenchcoat and her father's shoes. Isn't that something? I can't forget it. And my mother, her mother, her father, and some other women were walking around her, made a circle around her, because—I don't know— either she would deliver the baby soon, or they didn't want the SS to see her. I don't know. And she never complained, she never asked for water or anything.

Years and years later when I had my own children, all of a sudden she came to mind. I mean all that time it was just like everything else, but when I became pregnant, all of a sudden Rachel's face was always in front of me. What happened to her. Because when we walked to the trains, there again like I said before, if you would be here that minute and not there, I wouldn't be here now. We were at the train station, and there must have been thousands of people sitting and waiting for the train.[2]

Because Sally H. and her sister, together with about a dozen other young girls, were randomly chosen by the SS to go to a nearby farm to work in the fields, she was not there when the others were deported that night, although she remembers hearing their screams. She and her sister were subsequently shipped to Skarżysko, and they were still alive when the war ended. Her parents did not return, but together with the pregnant Rachel were gassed in Auschwitz.

Like Mado, Sally H. cannot simply celebrate the birth of her child because in her imagination she associates it with the doom of Rachel and her unborn infant. She suffers from what I call a tainted memory, and neither the passage of time nor an unwilled amnesia can erase it. There may be a valid text about small communities of women who survived through mutual support or some strength of gender, but it exists within a darker subtext emerging in these testimonies. To valorize the one while disregarding the other is little more than an effort to replace truth with myth.

Yet witnesses are often reluctant to forgo the option of a dignified gendered response. This reluctance can result in a clash between texts and subtexts that frequently remains unnoticed as the auditor engages in what we might call selective listening, in search of proof for a particular point of view. A classic example is the testimony of Joly Z., who lost all her family in Auschwitz except her mother, with whom she remained despite a transfer to Hamburg and then Bergen-Belsen, where they were liberated by the British in April 1945. She insists that the mutual support between mother and daughter enabled both to survive, and she ends with a little homily about the duty of asserting moral responsibility in the camps no matter what the conditions.

Embedded in her testimony, however, is a subtext, what I call a durational moment, that challenges her main text and reminds us how complex is the task of judging gendered behavior when painful circumstances like the following deprive one of the freedom to enact moral responsibility:

> JOLY Z.: There was a pregnant woman among us. She
> must have been in a very early pregnancy when she got
> in the camp. Beautiful woman. I remember her eyes
> always shining. Maybe the very fact that she had a life
> within herself gave her this extra energy and hope, to
> want to survive. But the time had come and she had to

deliver, and in the washroom they prepared a bed for her, and I was assisting . . . .

INTERVIEWER: In Auschwitz?

JOLY Z.: No, this was not in Auschwitz, this was already in Hamburg. And I was assistant to the doctor there, and that was a prisoner doctor. And I prepared the little box with some soft rags for the baby. And in the other room I heard suddenly the cry of the baby. I never saw or remembered before a newborn baby. And I was waiting for the baby with the little box in my hands. And then a tall SS man brought out the baby holding him or her upside down. And put it under the sink, and opened the water, and he said, "Here you go little Moses, down the stream." And drowned the little baby.

INTERVIEWER: What did you do?

JOLY Z.: For a long time, for a long time, it was very difficult to have hope after that.[3]

Compassion plays a negligible role here. The ritual of childbirth may be defined by the witness's expectations, based on her innocent sense of what should happen, but the outcome is decided by the SS, who sees both mother and child, and the witness, too, as victims of a specific doom, not agents of their own fate. When the miracle of giving birth and killing in the same time became the rule rather than the exception for the actresses in this familiar drama, events beyond their control mocked their efforts to create for themselves a gendered part.

Indeed, in some instances, women were forced to *reject* what they regarded as one of their natural roles as a result of their ordeals in the camps. Consider the testimony of Arina B. She was married in the Warsaw ghetto in 1941. The following year, she and her husband were deported to Treblinka, but on the journey he managed to tear the wire grate from the window, help her out, and leap after her. Others who tried to get out were shot, but they managed to escape. They lived for a while with local farmers, then returned to Warsaw to stay on the Aryan side, but were finally drawn back within the ghetto's walls by a desire to visit her parents and his brother. Subsequently, she was sent to Majdanek, and then to Auschwitz. Her narrative moment begins:

> The worst—you know, the worst part of my being in
> concentration camp, my nine months' pregnancy. I was
> pregnant when I came to camp. In the beginning I didn't
> know that I'm pregnant, nobody knew. But when I find
> out . . . it's hard to understand what I went through.
> Especially the last days, when the child was pushing to
> go out, and I was afraid I'm gonna make on the—you
> know how we call the beds, you know the bunk beds,
> and they're gonna beat me up. And I was so afraid
> because I got twenty-one [lashes] in Majdanek. And all
> the time my body was, you know, blue, my whole body
> was blue. I was afraid of beating because I didn't want to
> be crippled. I said to myself, if something—let them
> shoot me, you know, to finish my life, because it was
> very hard to live, very hard. Many times I was thinking
> to go on the wire, you touch it and just finish, but in the
> back of my head was "Who gonna tell the world what
> happen?" Always the same thing. . . .
> And when I came back one time from the outside, I
> got terrible pains, and we had midwife in the barracks,
> and she hear the way, you know, and she said to me,
> come out on the oven. You know, in the barrack was a
> great oven going through. I went out to the oven, and
> the baby was born. And she said, "You have a boy." And

she took away the boy, and till today I don't know where is the boy. I beg her, I hear crying, and I beg her to give me the baby. I'm very, I said "I don't want to live, I want to die with my baby, give me my baby. I don't have any, you know, I said I lost my, you know, strength and everything, I can't fight any more, I want to die. And she look at me, and she sit down, and she beg me to quiet up, and she said: "You're so beautiful. You're gonna find your husband. You're gonna have children, still children." I still remember the words what she told me. I said, "I can't live any more. I want to die. And till now I don't know where's my baby."[4]

How shall we read this narrative? That in the camps, women helped each other to survive? My earlier mention of the role that the "missed destiny of death" plays in the memories of witnesses receives concrete expression here. In the chaotic scheme of values created for their victims by the Germans, a birth moment is a death moment, and a mother's ambition is to leave her life to join her murdered infant. In the dialogue between hope and despair that we have just heard, nothing remains to praise. Whose spirit can the midwife's soothing words gladden?

But Arina B.'s story doesn't end here. She continues:

I was lucky. I find my husband after the war. I didn't know for three months if he's alive, but I count on two people—my sister and my husband. And they're alive . . . I find my husband. And finally we made home in Marburg an der Lahn in Germany. And I was so afraid to have a child; he wants family. And I said: "for what? Again gonna happen, again gonna kill our children?" I was so afraid always. And I got my son. I was pregnant with second child and I didn't want it. I was afraid again. And I said to my husband, "I don't want to have a child any more. I hate to be in Germany; I hate all the Germans. I can't stand these stones, covered with blood, everything is in blood." And I was so . . . if he was thinking to have a baby, I was angry at him. And I said, "Fine, I'm going to look how to get rid of it, the baby." And I went, I got rid.[5]

The chronological text of Arina B.'s story has a happy ending, as her midwife in Auschwitz proves to have been a subtle prophet. Six years after coming to the United States, Arina B. had another child, and she now salutes with pleasure her two beautiful children and four grandchildren. But almost in the same breath, she furnishes a durational subtext, unwittingly internalizing her own image of stones covered in blood: "I'm like stone," she reports, "sometimes I feel I'm stone—inside, you know."[6] We are left with a complex portrait of a woman who has survived an unspeakable ordeal to pursue a normal life while simultaneously abnormal death continues to pursue her. Although her previous "homes" include Majdanek, Auschwitz, and Ravensbrueck, she has adapted far better than Charlotte Delbo's Mado; however, we must still face the dilemma of defining vitality for a witness who calls herself a woman of stone.

The testimony of Shari B. gives us a vivid glimpse into how circumstances could curtail the independent spirit of a young girl between her seventeenth and eighteenth years, a spirit that under normal conditions would certainly have flourished with a decided feminist flair. Arrested by the Gestapo while living in Bratislava with false papers, she is interrogated and beaten at night and during the day forced to clean out the police officials' offices. One afternoon, she approaches a window on the second floor and is wondering whether to jump out when an officer enters and says, "Are you thinking of jumping? I can put you out of your misery right now, if you want." He aims a pistol at her head, and she remembers thinking, "If I faint, they will surely kill me," so she tells herself: "This moment will pass. This moment will pass." Finally, he puts the gun away, saying, "I don't want to cause a mess in the office. They're going to shoot you like all of the Jews anyway."

Eventually, she is deported to Theresienstadt. Her determination not to let the Germans kill her is tested further on the journey when she tries to climb through the small window of her boxcar. The other people in the car pull her back, arguing, "If you escape, they'll come and shoot us." A fracas ensues among the prisoners, and Shari B. remembers turning to them and crying, "You are old; you are all old and have lived your life already, but I am young and want to go on living." Fear is a powerful deterrent to community spirit, however, and the illusion that one woman's survival can be isolated from the potential death of innumerable others can be maintained only by ignoring the inroads that German terror made on the individual will.

In spite her inner resolve to resist, in Theresienstadt, Shari B. is reduced to the demeaning state of utter vulnerability, a situation that many women report as worse than the threat of death. She and the other women in her barrack are lying around naked when some SS men start walking through the room. She weeps as she speaks: "We were dehumanized. This was our most humiliating moment and I hated them that they should be able to walk around and see us naked." But there was nothing she could do. The episode is clearly seared on her memory, as she relives it still overwhelmed by shame and hatred.

This is bad enough, but in Shari B.'s narrative we have an instance of how her ordeal lingers on in the response of her son. She and her husband had left Czechoslovakia and come to the United States after the war, but he died young of lung cancer, leaving her with two small children to raise:

Once I read a report that children of Holocaust victims are affected, and I asked them [her children], "How do you feel about this? Do you feel you are affected?" And they said, "Mommy, how can you ask such a question? Of course we are affected!" And I said, "But you know, I never really told you anything as long as you were little." And they said, "Yes, but do you think we didn't know every time someone spoke about Germans or so on, you always had a comment."

And then I recalled an incident that happened. My son went to school, he was about six and a half or seven, and at school they must have told him about the Holocaust. And he came home, and he raised his hand and said "Heil Hitler!" And I did not say anything, but I said, "You know Robbie, don't ever say that." And he became very serious, and he didn't ask me why not. He went to the bathroom, and wouldn't come out for quite a while, and . . . . So I would knock, and said, "Now what are you doing there? Come out please." And he came out, and his hand was bleeding, and so I said, "How did you hurt it, what happened?" And he said, "I scratched it out, so I should never say it again."

So I don't know. I didn't tell him anything. I felt I never really spoke to them while they were little, yet I must have conveyed something.[7]

Holocaust testimony is not a series of links in a chain whose pattern of connections can be easily traced but a cycle of sparks erupting unpredictably from a darkened landscape, teasing the imagination toward illumination without ever offering it the steady ray of stable insight. My final fragment of women's witnessing probes how Edith P., who, as she says, has a wonderful family but no past, strives to merge her memories of Auschwitz into her present life. In the course of her meditation, she accents for us the delicate balance between gender and human identity, and the tension between personal and cultural origins of the self, that surface in so many of these oral narratives:[8]

> I just want to say, I've been liberated thirty-five years, going to be this month—April fourteenth [1980]. And as I get older, and my children are all self-sufficient and no longer at home, and I am not busy being a mother and a wife, and I can be myself—I have given a great deal of thought how I should conduct myself vis-à-vis the Germans, how I should feel. Should I hate them? Should I despise them? Should I go out with a banner and say, do something against them? I don't know; I never found the answer. And my own soul . . . and I have to go according to my own conscience—I cannot conduct myself [by] what my husband tells me or my children, or what the world has said. The only thing I can say is that up until now I ignore them. I don't hate them. I can't hate. I feel I would waste a lot of time in my life. But sometimes I wish in my darkest hours that they would feel what we feel sometimes, when you are uprooted, and bring up children—I'm talking as a mother and a wife— and there is nobody to share your sorrow or your great happiness. Nobody to call up and say something good happened to me today: I have given birth to a beautiful daughter; or she got all "A"s; she got into a good college. I mostly remember when holidays come, I have tried to preserve the holidays as I saw it at home, transfer it to my own children. We have beautiful Passovers like I saw it at home. But the spirit is not there. It's beautiful, my friends tell me, when I invite them that it's beautiful, it's very spiritual. But I know it's not the same. I . . . I . . . there's something missing. I want to share it with someone who knows me really.[8]

"I am no longer busy being a mother, a wife, and I can be myself"—under other circumstances, we might applaud this as a triumphant liberation of the pure feminine spirit from more traditional and, for some, confining activities. But how can we say that in this case? Edith P.'s Holocaust experience has undermined the rhetoric of renewal and self-discovery. The subtext of her life and her testimony is not a quest for release but an admission of irreplaceable loss. What she calls her absent past is permanently present *inside* the woman who is utterly alone at a Passover seder despite the company of her husband, her children, and her friends.

The curtailed potential of her stillborn life as a sister and a daughter, or her incomplete life as a wife and mother, because she is cut off together with her husband and children from the family she cannot share with them, leaves her a legacy of internal loneliness that nothing can reverse. But if we substitute for these gendered terms the more generic ones of parent and child, we move Edith P. and the other women I have been discussing into a human orbit that unites them through a kind of regret that cannot be sorted by sex. To be sure, pregnancy and childbirth are biologically unique experiences, and we have heard how they have been endured under unbearable conditions. But if we examine the following brief, complex moment of testimony, involving not only a wife, husband, and infant but also the daughter of the witness by a second marriage, we may glimpse the danger of overstating the importance of a biologically unique experience. The family is awaiting deportation, and the witness records the feeling of utter helplessness that seized so many victims at moments like these:

> This was summer. Outside there was a bench. So we sat
> on the bench, my wife holding the kid [their infant
> child] in her arms. In my head, what to think first of.
> You want to do something, and you know you're in a
> corner. You can't do *anything*. And when somebody asks

me now, "Why didn't you fight?" I ask them "How would *you* fight in such a situation?" My wife holds a child, a child stretches out [its] arms to me, and I look at him, and she says "Hold him in [your] arms, you don't know how long more you'll be able to hold him. . . . " [The witness sobs with remembered grief, as his daughter from his second marriage, who is sitting next to him on the couch, puts a consoling arm around her father and leans her head on his shoulder.] Me, a man, crying.[9]

Exactly like Edith P., Victor C. might protest, "I have a family, but no past," and could we reasonably argue that there is a gendered difference between the two expressions of anguish? The origins of humiliation were often dissimilar for men and women, because womanhood and manhood were threatened in various ways. But the ultimate sense of loss unites former victims in a violated world beyond gender. Victor C. clings to his daughter in the present, but the subtext of his life is the moment when, as the member of an earlier family, he was separated from his wife, his child, his mother, and his grandmother, all of whom were shipped to Auschwitz and gassed. Shall we celebrate the fact that because he was a man, and able to work, his life was saved? I think that he, a man crying, would not agree.

In the testimonies I have studied, I have found no evidence that mothers behaved or survived better than fathers, or that mutual support between sisters, when possible, prevailed more than between brothers. We do have more accounts of sisters staying together than brothers, but that is probably because brothers were more often separated by the nature of the work they were deemed able to do. This is an example of situational accident, not gender-driven choice. In all instances, solicitude alternated with frustration or despair, as the challenge of staying alive under brutal conditions tested human resources beyond the limits of decency—although we hardly need to mention that the victims shared no blame for their plight.

As for the ability to bear suffering, given the unspeakable anguish with which all victims were burdened, it seems to me that nothing could be crueler or more callous than the attempt to dredge up from this landscape of universal destruction a mythology of comparative endurance that awards favor to one group of individuals over another. The pain of loss and the relief of survival remain entwined in the memory of those lucky enough to have outlived the atrocities. All efforts to find a rule of hierarchy in that darkness, whether based on gender or will, spirit or hope, reflect only our own need to plant a life-sustaining seed in the barren soil that conceals the remnants of two-thirds of European Jewry. The sooner we abandon this design, the quicker we will learn to face such chaos with unshielded eyes.

FOUR

The Alarmed Vision
Social Suffering and Holocaust Atrocity

Until we find a way of toppling the barrier that seques-
ters mass suffering in other regions of the world from
the comfort and safety we enjoy far from its ravages, little will be
done to rouse the attention of our political or professional leaders,
to say nothing of our own. Domestic calm encourages distancing
from foreign pain. Past episodes of catastrophe like the Holocaust
have taught us how difficult it is for the distress of others to disrupt
the tranquil rhythms of our daily lives. We may be horror-struck
by the chaos that starvation and civil strife inflict on victims in
foreign places like Somalia or Sarajevo, but to be horror-struck is a
frugal form of charity. We need, but lack, a new kind of discourse
to disturb our collective consciousness and stir it into practical
action that moves beyond mere pity.

I think we will get nowhere with this problem until we admit
that the familiar verbal modes for approaching it have been exhausted by centuries of repetition. Even a word like "suffering"
does little to help us imagine the modern disasters we are challenged to confront. In fact, by calling the murder of European
Jewry an example of mass suffering, we risk narrowing its scope by
merging it with prior models that are meager measures of the

event. Job endured loss but gained divine acknowledgment and a limited spiritual insight after refusing to let physical trial curtail his moral strength. Nothing could be further from the ordeal of the Holocaust victim than this prototype of unprovoked suffering, which is deemed redemptive only by those who misread Job's protest. The Gospel accounts of the passion of Jesus are equally useless in aiding us to visualize the dilemma of the Holocaust. So, too, are the fictional visions of Leo Tolstoy and Fyodor Dostoyevsky that draw so heavily on those narratives. The notions of moral rebellion, punishment, and salvation that energize such Old and New Testament texts do not lead us to the outskirts of Auschwitz or Treblinka, nor indeed to the atrocities in Bosnia-Herzegovina. They steer us instead into friendly harbors where neither conscience nor imagination is in any danger of running aground.

Holocaust literature is a major goad urging us to reimagine atrocity and to rewrite the text of suffering in contemporary terms. A brief poem by Israeli writer Dan Pagis is a classic example of such artistic provocation:

Written in Pencil in the Sealed Boxcar

Here in this transport
I am Eve
With Abel my son
If you should see my older son
Cain son of man [or Adam]
Tell him that I[1]

The journey from the Garden of Eden to the gas chambers of Auschwitz bears no scriptural authority, but because deathcamps need no biblical model to confirm their existence, it is Scripture and not history, according to Pagis, that must alter its text. A Siamese bond now twins creation with destruction in a way that sabotages the narrative of Cain's primal crime and replaces it with a story of mass murder. This in turn imposes new burdens on our very notion of Scripture and its role in the unfolding human saga.

But the poem does much more. Because Genesis is a completed tale, the reader is coaxed to demolish its frame and through a kind of imaginative osmosis inject into its ancient nucleus a new vision more consistent with results it could not have foreseen. Who could have predicted for Eve and her issue the voyage that would turn Abel into a different kind of victim and fraternal violence into a vast catastrophe? The loss of a single son was the start of the Jewish narrative; the murder of an entire people was the beginning of something else, though we are left uncertain of what because Eve's unspoken message is buried in the challenge of her arrested voice. Whatever its content might have been, it would have included a summons to the alarmed vision, a call to Cain (and the rest of us) to rethink his assigned role and through a retroactive gesture of spiritual insight, somehow assimilate the dreadful end that awaits his mother and his brother into one of the archetypal chronicles of Jewish destiny.[2] A poem can no longer balance through its achieved form the void of discord that recent history seems to offer us. Deprived of this common solace from art, we are invited by Pagis to join in the perilous ritual of closure without any pledge that our search for meaning will uncover new comforts to blunt our grief.

The shift from fratricide to genocide as the norm of violence in the modern era is not easy to absorb. Not long ago I was engaged in a discussion with a historian who disputed my claim that the United States's lethargy in response to the plight of the Jews just before and during World War II resulted largely from a failure of imagination, a refusal or inability to etch on some internal monitor the details of the calamity that was consuming European Jewry. He argued that by 1942 Washington had "knowledge" of the deathcamps and "confirmed" reports that the mass murder was under way. Actually, Americans had such information as early as the summer of 1941, when German mobile killing units in the Soviet Union began systematically executing the Jewish population in areas the army had conquered. "Confirmed knowledge," however, is a verbal expression that does little to threaten the repose of a mind outraged from a distance and privy simply to the data that telegrams, communiqués, and written summaries can convey.

It seems to me a little naive to expect governments and citizens to react with dispatch to accounts of disaster that are couched in general language, lacking specific facts. When Gerhardt Riegner, head of the Geneva office of the World Jewish Congress, learned on August 1, 1942, from a sympathetic German industrialist with connections in the Nazi hierarchy that a plan had been reviewed in Hitler's headquarters for the murder of all Jews in Nazi-occupied lands, Riegner promptly sent this information to Rabbi Stephen S. Wise in the United States, who passed it on to the State Department. This was eight months *after* the first killing center had been opened at Chelmno in Poland. Instead of delaying interminably while "verifying" and then pigeonholing such stories, would the State Department have acted with a greater sense of urgency if Riegner had been able to describe how the Jews at Chelmno who were gassed in vans with carbon monoxide on the way to the site of mass burial sometimes arrived stunned instead of dead but were thrown into the graves anyway and buried alive? Would the response have been different if he had been able to tell about the Jewish worker at Chelmno who, when he opened one of the vans, pulled out the corpses of his wife and two children, and leaped into the grave beside their bodies asking to be shot and buried with them? (The Germans dragged him out, declaring that *they* decided when a Jew was to die.)[3] Of course, Riegner didn't have these details, though similar evidence was given to the Polish underground by two women who had escaped from Chelmno, and it was transmitted to the Polish government in exile in London. It probably was not believed. But it seems clear to me that the meaning and impact of an expression like "confirmed knowledge" depends on how that knowledge is being confirmed and on the language used to confirm it.[4]

Those who tried to summon Americans to action on behalf of the victims faced a double impasse: they lacked a vocabulary designed to portray the moments of atrocity I have just related; and they addressed an audience unable to hear because their mindset was not tuned, and had never been tuned, to the kind of crisis that was unfolding in Europe at that very moment. Even the Christian courier Jan Karski, who had visited the Warsaw ghetto twice, had spent a few hours disguised as an Estonian guard in the Belzec deathcamp, and then was sent by the Polish underground to England and the United States to give an eyewitness account, could not impress on the skeptical minds of Anthony Eden, Felix Frankfurter, and Franklin Delano Roosevelt the enormity of the crimes being committed against the Jews and the absolute necessity of finding some way of limiting the murders.[5]

The fact is that the system of values cherished by the American mind, with its stress on individual success and an infinitely improving future, nurtures a psychology of mental comfort that discourages encounters with tragedy, to say nothing of the minutiae of atrocity that an event like the Holocaust requires us to absorb. But in the case of the Holocaust, this attitude was not confined to a particular culture. Even the intended victims were unprepared to handle the tales of slaughter that drifted back to the ghettos from the killing centers. Abraham Lewin, in his *Diary of the Warsaw Ghetto,* drafts the dilemma of digesting "confirmed knowledge" of the unthinkable in the heart of the maelstrom:

> Isolated refugees who arrive here literally by miracle
> from Treblinka bring reports that freeze the blood in the
> veins. The killing-machine there never rests. In the past

few days Jews from Radomsko were brought there and murdered. News of this kind causes us hellish torments. Has anyone ever described the suffering of someone who has been condemned to death and who is to go to the gallows? Even the Russian artists, of whom the greatest is Dostoevsky, have not succeeded in giving a true description of what transpires in the depths of the soul of an innocent person who has been sentenced to death. When I hear these accounts of Treblinka, something begins to twist and turn in my heart. The fear of "that" which must come is, perhaps, stronger than the torments a person feels when he gives up his soul. Will these terrible agonies of the spirit call up a literary response? Will there emerge a new Bialik able to write a new Book of Lamentations, a new "In the Town of Slaughter"?[6]

In calling for a new Book of Lamentations, Lewin, like Dan Pagis, dismisses old scriptural models as sources of inspiration for portraying the murder of European Jewry. The quest for analogy, whether by literary artist or historian, is the task that bedevils anyone aiming to initiate the imagination of an unwary audience into the singular realm of the unthinkable. The crime of our century, as Lewin predicts here, will be the chronic story of men and women and children trying to stay alive in an environment that is moving them relentlessly toward a barbarous death that bears no relation to their previous lives. How does one describe the "fear of 'that' which must come" so as to differentiate it from ordinary dying?

In a desperate effort to make sense of his grim surroundings, Lewin himself is drawn in two directions at once. On one hand, he lapses into the language of consolation, born of the psychology of mental ease, to deflect implications too horrible to admit: "It is impossible that so much innocent blood should be spilled without retribution. The day of judgment, the day of reckoning must and will come." But it never came. The habit of taking refuge in such rhetoric when one is left powerless to change one's situation is understandable, and Lewin seems aware that he is doing this, because virtually in the same breath he adds a contrary idea: "The level of Nazi brutality quite simply lies beyond our power to comprehend. It is inconceivable to us and will seem quite incredible to future generations, the product of our imagination, over-excited by misery and anger" (81). But the "inconceivable," in this case as well as in subsequent instances of mass violence in the post-Holocaust period, is nothing more than a name for a reality that we are unprepared to accept, because it either offends our sense of order or threatens to unravel the curtain before which we ply our daily lives.[7]

If some forms of human misery do indeed still lie beyond our powers to comprehend, it would be irresponsible to allow our psychological and intellectual hesitation to estrange us from that misery. The only alternative, a complex and difficult one, is to find ways of making the inconceivable conceivable until it invades our consciousness without meeting protest or dismay. Drowning in daily episodes of atrocity, Lewin responds to the *experience* of his muted tongue and stunned imagination, not to a rhetorical invocation of silence. A "new Bialik" would have to abandon, not rediscover, the literary techniques and imaginative vision of his predecessors. But such rejection might introduce a chaotic rupture into some of our most cherished views, like time as uninterrupted chronology or history as automatic progress—a rupture that many commentators are loath to embrace.[8]

In classical Greek literature the herald led a perilous life, because as a bearer of ill tidings he so often provoked the wrath of the recipient of his message. When the escaped messenger from Treblinka brought the evil news that the Germans were gassing all the Jews and throwing their bodies into flaming pits, he was not punished but simply rebuffed as a madman by most members of the

Jewish Council. Oddly, individuals and communities clamor for more stories of extraordinary *virtue*, no matter how exaggerated: holy sightings and unlikely miracles quickly rouse public enthusiasm while the locales of the supposed events are soon turned into sacred shrines. But an unholy world with millions of victims and few heroes has little popular appeal because it proves inhospitable to the romanticizing imagination. We need to defend ourselves against reports of such radical evil. "Inconceivable" becomes a frightful word chiefly when it refers to atrocities like the Holocaust that offer us no possibility for transcendence. Such verbal threats prompt us to build bunkers of inner security to shield us from their assault.

It may be useful to *classify* human misery in terms of social problems, but this rarely generates widespread concern. We need a special kind of portraiture to sketch the anguish of people who have no agency in their fate because their enemy is not a discernible antagonist but a ruthless racial ideology, an uncontrollable virus, or, more recently, a shell from a distant hillside exploding amid unsuspecting victims in a hospital or a market square. In other words, before we can present a program for dealing with human misery, we need to *represent* that misery. This requires talents that will not flinch from physical outrages bearing no resemblance to the sufferings of an earlier era or from horrors untempered by moral meaning, whether plague or poverty or war, which were so often allied to a language of sanctity, virtue, or sentimental fervor.

Those talents include not only a verbal facility but frank consent to a philosophical shift about human expectation that allows us to work with limited aspirations, rather than the unlimited ones bequeathed by our Enlightenment and Romantic heritage. Unfortunately, what I call the alarmed vision feeds on a skimpy diet, one that fails to satisfy the appetite of those who "normalize" violence, disease, and other affronts to human dignity by placing them in the simple context of an agenda for improving the future. Few regard with enthusiasm the spectacle of diminished promise that the repeated abuses of our era have thrust upon us. The pragmatic decision to choose "reconciliation" over justice in places like Argentina, Chile, Haiti, and South Africa (to be followed, perhaps, by Rwanda and Bosnia-Herzegovina) creates a dubious legacy for the worldwide victims of brutality and an even more doubtful precedent for those who would seize and misuse power in the future. Defusing alarm by deflecting atrocity may create a fragile peace in communities wearied by seemingly endless periods of anguish, but it would be less than honest to ignore the price we pay for such a strategic form of avoidance.

Such avoidance resembles the attitude of those who use the texts of Holocaust testimonies as examples of "working through" past traumas toward a goal of reconciled understanding and a liberating growth into the future. But the subtexts of those testimonies reveal a reality that is much more relevant to the issues we are exploring here. They reflect hundreds of instances of unredeemed and unredeemable loss, giving us a glimpse of how language shorn of a spiritual bond can shock the imagination into an alarmed vision—the only kind of vision that may goad us to intercede in situations of atrocity before they have spent their energy, leaving negotiated "reconciliation" as the only practical course of action. Such situations mock the good intentions of utopian hopes. They introduce us to a reversal of expectation that lies at the heart of any attempt to appreciate modern suffering. The Holocaust and subsequent large-scale atrocities exist in an orbit void of the usual consoling vocabulary: martyrdom, the dignity of dying, guilty conscience,[9] moral rigor, remorse, even a term like "villainy," which in literary tragedy so clearly distinguishes the victim from his or her persecutor. None of these verbal categories illuminate the devastation of the Holocaust, or for that matter the killing of millions by Josef Stalin in the 1930s by enforced famine, or the ravages in Cambodia, or the merciless destruction of civilian populations in Yugoslavia in more recent years.

In a world where the goal of life so often appears to be the death of others, we are forced to regard the reversal of expectations rather than the fulfillment of dreams as the model for being and behavior in some communities. Ironically, Nazi Germany nearly succeeded in establishing a prototype for this social paradigm by equating its extermination policies with the dream of a Third Reich cleansed of Jews. A healthy community thus became by definition one in which the death of some was decisively tied to the life of the remainder. Because such a system violates our moral and spiritual beliefs, we find it difficult, if not impossible, to imagine. But history pays little heed to what we find desirable or imaginable. The Holocaust and later atrocities have invaded our sense of stable living and normal dying, leaving us a legacy that colonizes the future with nightmares of frustration rather than dreams of fulfillment.

It would help to be able call this condition a treatable trauma, but if the testimonies of hundreds of Holocaust survivors are to be trusted, that clinical formula simply will not serve the truth of their ordeal. As we shall see, their memories are not symptoms, nor in telling their tales do they seek some form of reintegration into their community—a goal they have long since achieved. Well-intentioned intervention after the fact is no substitute for strong action to prevent atrocities from occurring. Painful memories are not always disabling, and narratives about them—at least this is true of Holocaust testimony—rarely "liberate" witnesses from a past they cannot and do not wish to escape. For them, forgetting would be the ultimate desecration, a "cure" the ultimate illusion. As for renewal or rebirth, such monuments to hope cannot be built from the ruins of a memory crammed with images of flame and ash.

The myth that such a patient needs to be freed from his or her past originates in a number of questionable assumptions. The first is the designation "patient," which immediately creates a clinical relationship and transforms testimony into a form of therapy. The second is the premise that survivors of atrocities experience time only chronologically, so that the present appears to follow the past and precede the future. Testimony may *sound* chronological to an auditor or audience, but the narrator who is a mental witness rather than a temporal one is "out of time" as he or she tells the story. This is often the case in Holocaust discourse; we are led astray or baffled by the lack of a language to confront the difference between the chronological current, which flows until we channel it between the permanent banks of historical narrative, and durational persistence, which cannot overflow the blocked reservoir of its own moment in memory and hence never enters what we call the stream of time.

Anyone who hears these testimonies will understand that for the witnesses time is durational as well as chronological and that durational time is experienced continuously, not sequentially as a memory from which one can be liberated. The notion that a Holocaust survivor—I suspect one might say this of any atrocity survivor—can generalize his or her personal suffering and move beyond the role of victim derives from an unfamiliarity with how durational time assails the memory of a witness. That is why I believe all attempts to investigate the effects of atrocity on a group or a community must begin with the narratives of individual victims, and especially with moments of durational time like the following, which mock the very idea of traumas that can be healed.

The speaker is Bessie K., a woman who is being interviewed with her present husband, also a survivor. Their chronological story is familiar: they met after the war, married, came to the United States, raised a family, and have led happy and successful lives. But this offers no compensation for what they are about to tell, which gives us a glimpse of the role durational time plays in their memories and lives. During their testimony, they sit at opposite ends of the same couch, isolated and insulated, each dwelling in a series of durational moments that they share with no one but themselves. As so often in these testimonies, the crucial instants are those explaining not how one survived but how a member of one's family died. On their deepest level, these life stories are really death stories, which include the death of the self, in ways we still need to interpret. In these instances, a descriptive word like "suffering" seems a futile term, because its traditional associations with healing or a process for gaining moral maturity, to say nothing of conventional theological ideas like salvation and redemption, consign it to a lexicon of outmoded vocabulary. Any thought of legitimizing such "suffering" through treatment becomes an offense to the witness.

Bessie K.'s narrative is preceded by her husband's account of his farewell to his brother, ill with typhus, who was taken by the SS with other inmates from the camp infirmary and shot. She tries to enter into his distress by passing him a tissue, but he rejects it with a flick of the wrist, saying, "I don't need it." Then he tells of his brother's last gesture—giving him his shirt after saying, "I don't need it." The memory of his brother's death consumes him, shrouds him in a way that prevents intrusion, even from his wife. She then begins the story of her own unforgettable durational moment:

> I had a baby boy. [. . .] They took us to the buses, they
> brought us to a big airfield. And nearby were the trains,
> the cattle trains. And . . . I look back: I think for a while
> I was in a daze; I didn't know what was happening
> actually. I saw they [were] taking away the men separate,
> the children separate, and the women separate. So I had
> the baby, and I took the coat what I had, the bundle, and
> I wrapped [it] around the baby and I put it on my left
> side, because I saw the Germans were saying left or right,
> and I went through with the baby. But the baby was
> short of breath, started to choke, and it started to cry, so

the German called me back, he said in German "What do you have there?" Now: I didn't know what to do, because everything was so fast and everything happened so suddenly. I wasn't prepared for it.

To look back, the experience was—I think I was numb, or something happened to me, I don't know, But I wasn't there. And he stretched out his arms I should hand him over the bundle; and I hand him over the bundle. And this is the last time I had the bundle.

But as I look back, I don't think that I had anybody with me. I was alone, within myself. And since that time I think all my life I been alone. [Meanwhile, the camera pans to the other end of the couch on which she is sitting to settle on her present husband, Jack, whose face is a mask of grief and despair.] Even when I met Jack, I didn't tell Jack my past. Jack just find out recently. For me, I was dead. I died, and I didn't want to hear nothing, and I didn't want to know nothing, and I didn't want to talk about it, and I didn't want to admit to myself that this happened to me.

She is deported to Stutthof concentration camp, where she meets the doctor who had operated on her infected breast in the ghetto before her deportation. She continues: "And when [the doctor] saw me there she was so happy to see me, and right away she says 'What happened, where's the baby, what happened to the baby?' And right there I said 'What baby?' I said to the doctor 'What baby? I didn't have a baby. I don't know of any baby.'" Then she pauses for an instant, nods her head, taps her brow with a finger, and concludes, "That's what it did to me."[10]

This fragment of narrative illustrates as well as anything I know why we must be cautious when trying to compare examples of individual or community suffering with each other. Certainly there may be some overlap between the experience of this bereft mother and of parents who have lost children more recently through acts of extreme violence in locales other than the Holocaust. But universalizing instances of atrocity only diminishes their private impact. Understanding the differences is crucial: the duration, nature, and extent of the violation, the role of the aggressor, the defensive resources available to the victims—issues like these enjoin us to view each atrocity within its historical, geographical, cultural, and psychological context. Some victims may indeed respond to treatment, may find group discussion useful, may need to escape from the cocoon of remembering that traps them in a corrosive past. But Bessie K. fits none of these models. When she says, "since that time I think all my life I been alone," while sitting next to her husband, she is not complaining or asking for sympathy; she is explaining that the passage of time cannot appease a durational memory. She is redefining the meaning of being "alone, within myself," making it a typical outgrowth of the disintegration of her first family, not to be undone by the emergence of a second one. The unappeasable experience is part of her inner reality, and though the optimistic American temperament winces at the notion, Bessie K. knows that what she has survived is an event to be endured, not a trauma to be healed.

But her narrative reveals even more. The Holocaust has collapsed conventional distinctions between living and dying as separate—indeed antithetical—states of being. We will never begin to understand the legacy of atrocity in the modern era until we realize what this means. When after telling of surrendering her baby Bessie K. insists, "For me I was dead. I died, and I didn't want to hear nothing, and I didn't want to know nothing," she invites us to reflect on a consequence of atrocity that surfaces in numerous survivor testimonies—the condition of having missed one's intended destiny by surviving one's death.[11] The death instant of her child is her own death instant, too, not in fantasy but in reality, a permanent intrusion on her post-Holocaust existence. It is also a form of verbal disturbance, since no language exists—certainly not a tame word like "suffering"—to describe the role of such durational moments in the lives of those who have outlived them.

Bessie K.'s durational moment is part of the normal experience of the deathcamp universe. If it seems abnormal or traumatic to us, that is because we approach it from our familiar perspective of chronological time. It is part not of her historical past but of her durational present, and as such is both unforgotten and unforgettable. She is defined, not disabled by her memory, a memory tellable but unshareable, because unlike loss through illness or accident, in her mind this was a "death" without parallel or analogy. It is neither desirable nor possible for her to "forget" it. Such expectations betray our need for amnesia, because narratives like hers threaten our dependence on coherence, reason, order, the moral and psychological balance that constitutes for us civilized being.

Testimony like this should summon us not to the healing of victims but to a revision of the myth of civilized being. Human nature can no longer be set in opposition to inhuman nature, as if one were the norm and the other a correctable aberration. Atrocity in the form of violence that maims and kills others has become a "normal" rather than a pathological expression of the self—not of all selves, to be sure, but enough to cause us to question ancient premises about moral instincts and spiritual purpose. In its display of power, the act of atrocity brings a fulfillment similar to the one we usually associate with gestures of charity or love. The tiresome cliché about people who do not learn from the past being doomed to repeat it persists as our favorite buffer against facing human and historical truth. Perhaps it is time to admit that atrocity in the past may not discourage but in fact *invite* atrocity in the future. From the scandalous carnage of World War I to the innumerable murders of the Leninist and Stalinist regimes to the countless victims of the Holocaust (condensed into a single abstract figure, six million) to the bloody outrages in Bosnia and Rwanda, our age of atrocity slips into and out of consciousness with the casual appeal of a transient news item. We fail to decipher the clues that would rouse us to an alarmed vision.

I am not sure that we can find a way of sensitizing this numbness, in whose protective custody we live to avoid the unsettling spectacle of the deaths of others. But I am sure that one useful beginning is with the voices of those who were plunged into a death-in-life milieu from which survival did not bring escape. The roots of the quandary began to appear in the camps themselves. One survivor of the liquidation of the Vilna ghetto (eleven years old at the time) who was sent with her mother to Kaiserwald near Riga tells of the kind of discussion she used to have with a friend in the camp:

> You kind of got laid back a little about being killed. The prime targets of our thoughts was always being killed. One of my friends [. . .] she and I went through—we met in Kaiserwald. She was from Liebau (people came there from Liebau too) and she and I were about the same age and conversations would be: "Let's see, how would you like to be killed? Would you like to be killed by the gas chamber? By being beaten? By hunger? Or the bullet?" And she and I agreed—the bullet. So our conversations were *not* building a future, what we are going to do when we grow up, you know how kids talk, I'm gonna be this and I'm gonna be that. Our hope was that when our time comes, that we will die by the bullet, so that we will suffer less.[12]

This is of course an extreme reaction to a death-stressed environment, but at the time other options for Jews seemed unlikely, and the witness is trying to recall her former state of mind honestly. It confirms my earlier remarks about the importance of reversal of expectation in contemporary thought, since the strategy focuses not on how to be happier but on how to suffer less. The most dramatic examples of what I call durational time in these testimonies invariably terminate in death, real or imagined, imagined not as fantasy or illusion but as a shared end that *should have been,* that does not violate but grows logically out of the present situation. What we think of as chronology, with its investment in a long-term future, had already died. For many inmates, the shrunken margins of space in the camps were accompanied by a contraction in the boundaries of time, and within that area of constricted space and time the planned doom of dying prepared for all potential victims by their persecutors scarred the memories of those who would be lucky enough to outlive that doom.

How else are we to explain the testimony of George S., who years after the event remembers with apprehension the challenges of ordinary life when he reentered chronological time? After his release from the camps he came to the United States, where he tried to settle into a normal pattern of existence. But because his life had been so *unsettled* during the war, he was left with a legacy of unresolved conflict that emerges starkly from this moment of his testimony. Following more than five hours of reviewing the destruction of all but one member of his extensive family, he abruptly begins to speak of his fear of marriage and starting a new family after such ruin. "A home," he defines, preparing for his narrative of how duration invades chronology, "is something you lose." This is a classic example of the reversal of expectation that an atrocity like the Holocaust has grafted onto our sense of modern reality. Nevertheless, he finds a job and marries. He has certainly earned an unimpeded future, but we are naive to anticipate this prospect. Unimpeded futures are now part of our nostalgia about the past. He reenacts in his dreams and even in certain physical responses during his waking hours the missed destiny of dying that still haunts him from the world of the deathcamps:

We bought a home, and started to establish ourselves, and things were getting better—but I had some drawbacks. I was working hard, trying to forget myself, forgetting the past, but it came back to me like a recording in my head. After we got married, for the longest time—we were already then in a family way, and things were looking up to me. During the day I was working hard, and studying, and trying to get ahead and establish myself—and at night, I was fighting the Germans, really fighting. And the SS were after me all the time, and I was trying to save my mother and my sister [gassed at Auschwitz]. I was jumping off from building to building, and they were shooting at me, and each time the bullet went through my heart. And I was sitting up not knowing at night in my bed, and I was screaming, you know it was hard on [my wife]. It must have been hard on her, and we didn't know how to handle it. I didn't know how to handle it. I was making believe . . . forgetting about it and going on during the day doing my things. And at night she was calming me down, she says "It's OK, it's OK, you're here, don't worry about it," and I was waking up and screaming at night and each time a bullet went through my heart.[13]

He returned to work, but his left arm began to pain him badly; he had difficulty driving the car, and one day a fellow worker rushed him to the hospital with the symptoms of a heart attack. The doctors found nothing physically wrong with him.

Is there such a feat as recharting your own death or, more precisely, perhaps, someone else's intention to kill you, so that the frustrated conclusion of durational time in the camps achieves some form of completion at a later date? The loneliness that surfaces as a theme in so many of these testimonies—like the mother who after surrendering her infant to the Germans declares, "Since that time I think that all my life I been alone," while sitting next to her husband—results from a separation caused by the murder of members of one's family, and that in turn leads to an internal rewriting of the scenario of life to somehow include one's death. Here agency invades necessity, defiance replaces inertia, and the victim by fighting the Germans and trying to save his mother and sister embraces and *earns* the death that has already devoured them. But his waking life thwarts this consummation devoutly to be wished, and his missed encounter with the destiny from which he escaped but so many others did not continues to exert its force as a subtext of his narrative.

Time does not close the gap between the text of his ongoing life and the subtext of his unpacified past, the unreconciled and un-reconcilable stress between chronology and duration. The issue grows even more dramatic if we turn to a 1993 *New Yorker* article addressing the problem of preserving the ruins of Auschwitz-Birkenau that time and nature are gradually eroding. The rem-nants of mass murder are also disintegrating, the mountains of human hair and suitcases and prostheses that stun the visitor into imagining the huge number of victims consumed by the insatiable death-machinery of the place. But the author cites an even more perplexing question mentioned by the deputy director of the Auschwitz museum: "Recently," she tells him, "a number of Holo-caust survivors have contacted us and asked that their remains be buried at Birkenau. . . . Birkenau is a cemetery," she adds, "but not a cemetery where you can conduct funerals."[14] For the moment, museum officials don't know what to do with this request, which seems grotesque only to those who ignore how the "missed des-tiny" of dying in Auschwitz continues to raid the memories of those who outlived their doom there. Together with George S.'s testimony, it reflects an ongoing need that many survivors feel to connect their lives to the death of others. This is the final reversal of expectation to disturb the serenity of our private consciousness, to say nothing of the smooth flow of chronological time. Few events have done more to create a tension between what we wish and what we know—if we allow ourselves to know it—than the atrocity of the Holocaust. The experience of its victims, those who survived and those who did not, permanently darkens the future by bequeathing us a legacy of unreconciled understanding. The passage of time heals many wounds, but this event leaves only a vexing and painful scab. No one is happy to discard the illusion that there is meaning in such suffering, that there is something to be learned from it, that the anguish of human cruelty can be minimized by calling it spiritual discipline. We live in an age haunted not by the kind of suffering that religion and literature have taught us to accept, but by a spectacle of atrocity, on smaller and larger scales, that no past traditions have prepared us to absorb. Thus any effort to aid its victims, on an individual or community basis, must begin by acknowledging that the usual consolations may not apply, that efforts to heal by forgetting the past and bravely facing the future might only betray a misunderstanding of the effects of atrocity on the human body, mind, and spirit.

Taking or watching Holocaust testimony is a humbling experience. You begin with the hope of creating order out of chaos, finding patterns in the survival narrative that can be organized into what some call a "syndrome." You imagine you can design a new template of evil to gain insight into the motives that lead to mass murder. Then you hear the story of a young Jewish woman who was thrust alive into the crematorium by two SS men because she refused to follow their order to undress and scratched one of them on the cheek when he tried to force her to do so. And suddenly your faith in the inviolable dignity of human nature collapses and you are left adrift on an alien sea without a moral compass. Exasperated by my own inability to envision anecdotes like the ones I was hearing in the testimonies, I revised my assumptions about shareable memory and collective consciousness. Once we enter the tentative world of duration, leaving behind the security of chronology, we realize that life after atrocity is not a call to new unity but only a form of private and communal endurance, based on mutual toleration rather than mutual love. This is much, though it is less than the utopia humanistic enlightenment once dreamed of achieving. All our efforts at rescue and remedy, nurture and renewal, must grow from this insight.

FIVE

Landscapes of Jewish Experience
The Holocaust Art of Samuel Bak

Painting, like literature, is a reciprocal art. A book without a reader is inert, stagnant, a candidate for extinction. Similarly, a painting without a viewer is a lifeless object, drained of kinetic force. Viewer and reader invest canvas and page with a vitality that draws its energy from the eye and the mind of an attentive human responder. We cannot look at the monumental paintings in Samuel Bak's "Landscapes of Jewish Experience" series without feeling the tension that slowly mounts as we grope to interpret their images. The shapes and spaces on the canvases first unite with each other, creating a fragile balance between substance and ruin. Then they leap forth to challenge us with the dual appeal of chaos and form, as we strive to populate the rubble with a living presence so visibly absent from most of the scenes before us.

Although all art requires active involvement, Holocaust art is especially demanding. Memory is a crucial catalyst in this process. The lack of human figures in most of Bak's forsaken landscapes will be a mystery only to those who ignore the incandescent shimmer that so often ripples through their atmosphere or the sinister smokestacks that rise like accusing fingers from a barren terrain. An unholy glow is all that lingers from millions of bodies consumed by fire. Among other possibilities, these paintings are dramatic bulwarks against amnesia. They are reminders of a sacred past, criminally besieged, crowded with emblems of a ravaged civilization. They contain fragments of a giant jigsaw puzzle called Creation that burden viewers with the task of retrieving its missing pieces while leaving them wondering whether those pieces may not have been lost forever.

To minimize the grimness of Bak's art is to falsify its content. "My paintings," Bak admitted more than a decade ago, convey "a sense of a world that was shattered, of a world that was broken, of a world that exists again through an enormous effort to put everything together, when it is absolutely impossible to put it together because the broken things can never become whole again. But we still can make something that looks *as if* it was whole and live with it. And more or less this is the subject of my painting, whether I paint still lives, or people, or landscapes, there is always something of that moment of destruction there. Even if I do it with very happy and gay colors, it has always gone through some catastrophe."[1]

What is "that moment of destruction"? Bak grew up in Vilna, the Jerusalem of Lithuania, a center of Yiddish learning that rivaled any in Europe. With the outbreak of war in 1939, the city was transferred from Poland to Lithuania. The Soviet Union occupied Vilna in June 1940, when Bak was a child of seven, and the Germans invaded a year later; from that point, the dismantling of Jewish culture and the destruction of Jewish life in Vilna began. When Russian troops reentered the city in July 1944, only a few thousand of the 57,000 Vilna Jews who had been subject to Nazi rule were still alive. Among them were Bak and his mother. His father had been shot a few days before the liberators arrived. The two ghettos, sole remnants of a once thriving Jewish community, lay in shambles.

This is the kind of personal legacy that stalks the "Landscapes of Jewish Experience." Bak's paintings comprise a visual testimony to the disaster, a profusion of images that admit us to an event many consider unimaginable. His canvases present relics of ruin and vestiges of order, a wasteland of Jewish tradition struggling out of its disarray, leaving his viewers to determine from this turmoil how much of a chance for renewal remains. A major strength of his vision is its refusal to commit to hope or despair. It reflects an art oscillating between expectation and dismay.

Alert viewers will notice in several of these paintings a *vov* and *gimel,* initial letters of the Vilna Ghetto, usually formed by odd scraps of wood and unobtrusively inserted into the visible text. They are cues to a vanished era, traces of a loss that is an unavoidable base for any effort to rebuild a future. Bak is much too honest a painter to pretend that survivors could turn toward rebirth while slighting their splintered past. The vistas that draw the eye into a distance of mountain peaks or sea and sky in many of these paintings beckon with an uncertain promise. The masses in the foreground, the colossal boulders and huge blocks of granite, the graves and tombstones and crumbling Tablets of the Law, weigh heavily on the imagination, discouraging an easy flight into an unfettered tomorrow.

The fate of the Vilna Ghetto and its inhabitants is a model for the doom of all of European Jewry. The familiar emblems of Jewish continuity—the Shabbat candles, the Star of David, the Ten Commandments—have not been vanquished, since they assert their presence even in the midst of a fretful gloom, but they declare themselves with a diminished vigor. Bak concedes the price the murderous Germans have wrested from the once sturdy symbols of Jewish existence while declining to grant final victory to the assailants. If he can be said to celebrate anything in this series, it is the stamina of the spirit of Jewish memory, affected and even afflicted by the powers of darkness, but never entirely annulled.

Bak has faced the Holocaust, both in its private and its public features, through what might be called a poetry of redefinition. Poetry thrives on images, on the dynamic dialogue among them

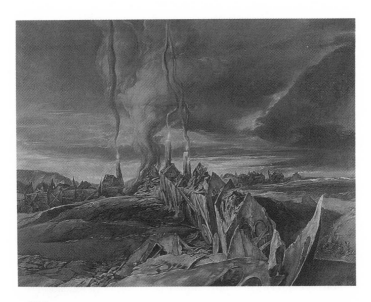

1. *Trains*

that stimulates a reader to a re-vision, and then a revision, of his or her prior sense of reality and of human experience. And this is precisely the lure of Bak's paintings. The so-called Final Solution has not extinguished Shabbat candles but forced them to light their sacred role in the shadow of the crematorium chimney. In *Trains* (fig. 1), smoke pours upward from the tips of the candle flames, inaugurating a profane Sabbath and evoking a "yahrzeit" that many would prefer to dismiss. And since the Holocaust, who can ever again regard a train merely as a conveyance for traveling from one place to another? Those familiar with Claude Lanzmann's *Shoah* will know how the train, in one of its incarnations, has been enshrined forever as a vehicle of death. Meanwhile, we have no way of deciding whether the ominous cloud in the right background is encroaching or dispersing, threatening the journey or welcoming it toward a brightness beyond the smoldering pyre near the center of the painting.

A poetry of redefinition involves an altered sense not only of images but of the lexicon that animates them, of the words and even the letters that grant us our means for noting the scenes around us. Bak gives us visual access to one of the basic principles of Holocaust art: it speaks to us with a language of tainted familiarity. The Ten Commandments have not lost their authority, but they address us now in a variety of tones, not excluding the ironic. "Do not murder" echoes with a hollow solemnity in a universe just awakening from the slaying of the people it was designed to enlighten. The role of the Divine Voice and its tokens of power and love is not revoked, but is summoned to a Joblike court of inquiry, as the ancient debate between the Lord and his people renews itself in a domain stained by the blood and ashes of European Jewry.

In none of these paintings is this anxious dialogue more vivid than in *From Aleph to X* and *Othyoth* (Letters), both reflecting the decisive holy moment when God sealed his covenant with the Jews in flight from Egypt by giving them the Ten Commandments. In *From Aleph to X* (fig. 2), two giant tablets loom over the ruin of a crushed Jewish community. They are firmly planted in the earth, like outcrops from some earlier eruption. At their base lies a partly demolished Star of David whose vague yellow tint reminds us of its faded glory. Beside it rises the emblem of its nemesis, a chimney belching pallid smoke, drained of its virile pigment, flattened against the tablet as if etched into its facade. If faith is to endure, must the Torah be "rewritten" to include the legacy of Auschwitz? Has the abused Star of David any hope of being restored to its former spiritual grandeur in the galaxy of Jewish belief?

These are momentous issues, not easily resolved. The immense tablets command the site like mastodons of Hebrew law, but the history of the Holocaust has not left them intact. In *Othyoth* (fig. 3) they have taken flight; unmoored from the landscape, they drift between sky and earth as if their future fortune must now be amended. What new revelation awaits us? The letters of the law,

2. *From Aleph to X*

no longer embedded in stone, float free, though we are left to imagine what has shaken them loose and what their unfixed status entails. As if bathed in divine radiance, a golden *aleph* crowns the picture, attesting the primacy of a revised text that has yet to be composed. Despite the vivid realism of the draftsmanship, the letters seem to have been cut from a celestial cover, a remnant of which may still cling to one of the crumbling tablets. Is this

3. *Othyoth*

dismembered alphabet returning to its source, or seeking a new earthly prophet, a post-Holocaust Moses to guide surviving Jewry beyond their primal heritage to repair the damage wrought by their modern catastrophe?

Such challenges may sound fanciful, but Samuel Bak is not the only Holocaust artist to raise them in his creations. There is no evidence that he has been a disciple of the Nobel Prize–winning poet Nelly Sachs, but anyone familiar with her verse will recognize an intimate kinship between the visions of the two. Her work helps us to appreciate the remarkable *literary* quality of Bak's achievement. The title of her first postwar volume, *In the Dwellings of Death,* and its initial poem, "O the Chimneys," signify the importance that a particular icon of disaster, so prominent in Bak's paintings too, plays in our imaginative response to the destruction of European Jewry. As post-Holocaust artists, they embrace a similar birthright, Sachs as a writer seeking to recover from the wounded word and Bak as a painter from the wounded image. But in a more complex sense, although their technical bents may differ, for poet and artist alike words and images are inseparable; the task of moving an audience between sight and insight is at once visual and cerebral. Words must be "seen," and images "read." Both artists share the conviction that the post-Holocaust bond between humanity and its spiritual future has turned enigmatic—one of Sachs's last series of poems is called "Glowing Enigmas"—launching for each of them a quest for new dimensions of perception. The context for this search is the impact that the slaughter of European Jewry has had on the sensibilities of the artist.

Anyone conversant with the deceitful speech and the fraudulent shapes devised to beguile Hitler's victims—"deportation" coded as "resettlement," gas chambers disguised as showers—will understand why the remolding of language and form are so important to the artistic imagination exploring ways to represent the calamity we call the Holocaust. The novel fusion of word with image is enshrined in the following plea from a poem by Nelly Sachs:

> do not destroy the cosmos of words
> do not dissect with the blades of hate
> the sound, born in concert with the breath.[2]

Bak might have said the same about the cosmos of images, especially those associated with the early vitality of Jewish tradition.

The need to protect familiar patterns from total annihilation drives Bak's creative energies, even as he charts a redesigned architecture of reality to contain them in a post-Holocaust universe.

The inspirations piloting Bak and Nelly Sachs at times seem identical, a resemblance all the more striking because during the war Sachs was in exile in Sweden. "The dreadful experiences that brought me to the very edge of death and eclipse," she wrote, "have been my instructors. If I had not been able to write [for which we might read 'paint'], I would not have survived. Death was my teacher. How could I have occupied myself with something else; my metaphors are my wounds. Only through that is my work to be understood."[3] Bak's metaphors are his wounds, too, throbbing and probably incurable, but paradoxically they proclaim a robust as well as an injured vision. His metaphors demand that we re-view, and then review, well-known models of spiritual consolation and consider how they may have been recast by secular ruin.

The painting *Shema Yisrael* (fig. 4) heralds an unorthodox message amid the havoc of a hallowed spot. Here the summit of a modern Sinai shines forth in surprising splendor, but only the name of the Lord is inscribed on the tablets at the peak. Strewn on the mountain's slopes, like shattered tombstones, is the wreckage of the earlier dispensation, the letters of their revelations scattered among the rubble like a jumbled text. The eye is drawn compulsively from a shadowed foreground to the blank tablets at the top, waiting to be engraved anew, presumably by a Divine Hand. Some sunlight seems to gleam through fleecy, drifting clouds. But the Chosen People are nowhere to be seen, their absence raising the unsettling question of how the effort to exterminate them has disrupted the ancient narrative of Genesis and Exodus.

Bak's metaphors may be read in many ways: this is a major source of their appeal. Semblances of the Ten Commandments wander through his paintings like leitmotivs from a Wagner opera. They lead an intertwined life, no single advent being indepen-

4. Shema Yisrael

dent of all the others. The viewing experience awakens musical as well as literary vibrations, each image enriching its fellows by a sequence of modulations, like the development of a symphonic theme, creating a synthesis of aesthetic response that draws on numerous arts. We do not trace the evolution of the artist's judgment as we move from painting to painting but endure instead the conflict of an incessant and unresolvable inquiry, variously displayed.

5. *Alone*

Nothing less than the destiny of the Jewish people is called into question, displacing with visual encounters that are fraught with memories of an agonizing past the logic that once led through thought to belief.

Such encounters create a space between painting and viewer that only interpretation can fill. In *Alone* (fig. 5), a citadel of stone molded like a Star of David (or a monstrous fish, or a gigantic rock fragment in the shape of a vessel about to break off from some adjacent shore) seems poised to launch itself into the brooding gloom of a cheerless sea. The hint of a distant radiance that il-lumines the surface of this floating island, one of Bak's unorthodox "still lives" from nature that more properly might be called "stilled lives," offers no assurance that this potential journey into a liquid wilderness will steer us to any kind of promised land. A leashed energy quivers between the almost defiant star, aimed like a strung arrow, and the ominous sky above. The density of the star, however, more sturdy than its feebler replicas in other of these canvases, does not make it any less forlorn in its solitude. This has often been the initial (though never the final) condition of survival for the Jewish people, the need to emerge from the ruins of their places of worship and habitation: the two Temples, Kristallnacht, the towns and villages and even ghettos of Europe that Jews once called home, the loneliness and wandering that has long been part of their historical pilgrimage.

Without explicitly depicting it, Bak has included in his "Landscapes of Jewish Experience" a focus for this legacy that remains the central spiritual site for the children of Israel, the Kotel, or Wall, in Jerusalem that together with the shattered fragments of the original Commandments remains the most sacred "Ur-ruin" of the Jewish imagination. But above and behind that holy place, where worshipers seal their prayers, lurk reminders of an unforgotten loss. In *Home* (fig. 6), the temple Wall forfeits its fixed place and becomes a transportable image; the imagination is forced to accustom itself to a strategy of multiple representation. The Holocaust like a palimpsest has imposed layers of further meaning on a once pristine religious iconography.

The shifting implication of images invites Jews to remember their culture *before* the Shoah and to absorb what it has done *to* their culture afterwards. The stones are at once threatening and innocent, rousing a cluster of associations that range from spiritual life to physical death. The wall in *Home* shields a humble dwelling in the foreground while hiding two menacing smokestacks behind. The eye is driven upward and outward in the dual motion that many of these paintings beseech: in a universe of hierarchy, the human spirit soars in the temple of the Lord on a journey toward God; while in the world of the Holocaust, the horizontal [secular] voyage of the Jews, by train or by foot, both eastward and westward, ends in destruction. Meanwhile, the smoke from the

6. *Home*

crematorium chimneys has infected the soothing appeal of hierarchy, since its ascent is freighted not with the hope of heavenly
peace but with a different and far more desolate kind of doom.

The shattered surfaces of sense and form in these paintings,
corresponding to a similar fragmentation of post-Holocaust reality,
conceal depths of intention, but we are obliged to pursue them with
a strenuous tenacity. In *Ghetto* (fig. 7), we have a clear reminder of

7. *Ghetto*

one personal origin of Bak's art: the *vov* and *gimel* entwined with the cloth Star of David is a signature of that inspiration. Beneath broken slabs of slate a crumbling community lies buried, crushed by a force too heavy to bear. As in all of these canvases, perspective is of foremost importance. There are no natural perimeters here to distract or console the viewer. The locus of attention is the center of the picture, where an underground tunnel beckons us into darkness and confusion. Those attentive to the history of the Vilna ghetto will know that the few resistance fighters who managed to escape must have fled through sewers beneath pavement something like this. We are asked to venture via the imagination on a perilous pursuit into the environs of Jewish fate, with no assurance that what we discover will bring any illumination.

This is perhaps the most exasperating dilemma for those who commit themselves to a study of one of the blackest moments in modern history. From this world of stone—curiously, many of the stories that form Tadeusz Borowski's *This Way for the Gas, Ladies and Gentlemen* are taken from a collection whose Polish title is *A World of Stone*—do we extract insight, or absence of meaning? The answer often depends on the *direction* of our encounter, the visual (and intellectual) line of sight that Bak so carefully imposes on his work, so that the eye and the mind fuse into the eye *of* the mind, leaving us unconsciously controlled by a viewpoint that leads from literal to figurative vision. If *Ghetto* plunges us into the depths of Jewish Holocaust experience, paintings like *Smoke* and *Flight* rise to its heights, but instead of trailing clouds of glory, as the romantic poet would have us believe, the spirits of the Holocaust dead have been tainted by an end that the Wordsworthian fancy could not have imagined. Although our vista is expansive in *Smoke* and *Flight* and not constricted as in *Ghetto,* issues raised by the connection to atrocity forbid us from embracing the free-floating masses near the center of these two paintings as metaphors of escape.

The link between Bak's originality and the literature of the Holocaust is once again forged by the parallel concerns of Yiddish poet Jacob Glatstein's "Smoke" and Bak's painting of the same name. Both poet and artist are anxious about the destiny of the Jewish soul after the disaster. Like Bak, Glatstein evokes a graveyard in the sky:

> From the crematory flue
> A Jew aspires to the Holy One.
> And when the smoke of him is gone,
> His wife and children filter through.
>
> Above us, in the height of sky,
> Saintly billows weep and wait.
> God, wherever you may be,
> There all of us are also not.[4]

Bak's sculptured cosmic cemetery, strewn with tombstones, is no New Jerusalem. Like the poet, the painter seeks a proper epitaph for his murdered fellow Jews. But earthly mourning is not enough. What is the role of God in this catastrophe? Do weeping billows in Glatstein's lines reflect divine tears, too? "How I love my unhappy God," he exclaims in another poem, "now that he's human and unjust." Implicit in both poem and painting are a riddle and an accusation, since both ponder the truancy of a once omnipresent God. Bak enters a treacherous region of inquiry with his solid stonescape floating on smoke. It images a "miracle" of potential negation, unmoored and adrift in a crippled universe that may have waived the option of personal intimacy with transcendent power—or transcendent love.

The paradox of presence known only through absence, the heritage of all Holocaust survivors who have lost their families, is enshrined in Glatstein's couplet: "God, wherever you may be / There also all of us are not." The missing victims, the missing meaning of their disappearance, the missing God to certify some solace for this awful drama of a blighted people, invade Bak's painting on a grander scale than they do Glatstein's minimalist poem. Blended pinks and blues haunt the atmosphere with an unsettling ghostly glow. The source of light is obscure, but the question *Smoke* (fig. 8) raises remains insistent, here and in many of its companion canvases: in a denatured world, disfigured by unnatural death, where is there room for the supernatural? Instead of distilling into spirit, smoke filters into the density of stone—a petrified and petrifying eschatology.

One of the many virtues and challenges of Bak's series is its ability to shape our reaction by altering mood and coloration from subject to subject. If *Smoke* confronts us with a solid mass set in a brooding sky, *Flight* (fig. 9) greets us with an evanescent panoply of nomadic fragments from an exploded culture, driven less by light than heat, whose source needs no explanation: a piece of prayer

8. *Smoke*

shawl, a striped rag-end of a camp prisoner's garment, paperlike facades from ruined Jewish dwellings—all weightless and lacking substance, just the reverse of the massive image central to *Smoke*. Surmounting these fragile relics are several Hebrew letters, also blown from their context, wafted on air without a text to give concrete meaning to their message. They spell "Shema" (Hear), but we are left to wonder who is the spokesman and who is ad-

9. *Flight*

dressed. Above the buoyant wreckage, the severed twin peaks of
the final letter *ayin* (**ע**) hover like two *yods* (**יי**), the traditional
designation for Adonai, the Lord. But the signs of God's name
have lost their original link to the language of Jewish prayer. Must
the alphabet of the covenant be written anew?

The poetry of redefinition that characterizes Holocaust art
casts forth this simple word and transforms its familiar appeal into

10. *Hidden Question,* diptych, left panel

a plea to a silent—or silenced—void. Is this the new *tohu vavohu,* the "waste and wild" of the post-Holocaust world, a diaspora in the firmament calling for a fresh creation from a previously unimagined chaos? Implicit in the title of the painting *Flight* is a memory bond with an earlier Exodus, but that journey was *toward,* not *from,* a promised land. In its modern guise, what will now fill the space between Genesis and Exodus, between "Shema" and the still unheard divine response? Job's protest provoked a Voice from the

11. *Hidden Question,* diptych, right panel

Whirlwind. What will succeed this ancient dispute over unjust anguish? Are these remnants of destruction bereft of consolation, doomed to wander like a missile off course in an empyrean desert eternally lacking guidance?

Although habitual frames of belief may have been damaged by the catastrophe, some uncommon ones remain. Certainly the "Shema" can be seen and heard by mortal eyes and ears. "Hear, O Israel," at least, remains a valid cry. Bak's works are a pledge against human blindness and deafness, and the curse of amnesia. Where the Holocaust is concerned, listening is a moral obligation, and remembering a spiritual act. Here, both unite into forms of seeing, first the literal viewing that we call sight, then the inward turning, the deepened thought we name insight, born of an active interplay between intellect and emotion. Art projects images that assume a life of their own and gain the special immortality that is granted to secular expressions of genesis, the act of creation. The "Landscapes of Jewish Experience" prompt us to think and to rethink that experience, reminding us that multiple viewpoints cannot merge into a single interpretation. The word "Shema," in its source and its target, embodies many voices. The ancestral flight from slavery to freedom mutates into a journey from atrocity to an uncertain destination. We now have two Jewish sagas to absorb, one starting with Creation, the other with Destruction: whether this is an inspiring or a desolate summons (or both) remains a central issue of these paintings.

That tension is reinforced by the diptych called *Hidden Question* (figs. 10, 11), where the mystery of divine purpose *and* presence is increased rather than solved by the rusted or broken keys that comprise a central motif in these adjacent paintings. The question mark in the handle of one key is balanced by the zero in the handle of the other, neither especially encouraging to our quest for meaning in a once divinely ordered universe. If we read from right to left, as Hebrew requires, then the stone arch burdening and shadowing the building—perhaps a synagogue—on the right seems shattered and dispelled in the canvas on the left, creating a buoyancy of weight and hue that suggests a casting off of bonds. Yet the name of Adonai, the twin *yods,* appears in both, a clue or an enigma that lingers above the Lord's temple but remains symbolically separated from the language of his people, the letters that allow a dialogue between them and insures a nurturing and covenantal role for their God.

The place of worship, or human dwelling, is restored intact.

Jews can gather there to renew their bond and to acknowledge the revival of their religious community. But in his visual inquiry into the state of post-Holocaust Jewish life, Bak refuses to simplify by celebrating partial victories. The name of God still perches on the stone fragments that once fused neatly into the Tablets of the Law, and the blank windows on the building in *Hidden Question,* shaped like these Tablets, remind us now of the need for a reinscription of faith. As the eye moves from right to left and back again, between a brooding darkness and a brightening day, we have an uneasy sense that before we can begin to solve some of the spiritual riddles raised by the murder of European Jewry, we must try to redraft our questions by plunging them into a new crucible of doubt.

The parallel masses in *Hidden Question* refuse to coalesce into a comfortable decree. The natural forms that crowd most of Bak's paintings are loath to disclose their secret. The viewer is faced with the need for redefinitions in nature that include the urge to re-fashion both the human image *and* the divine. Nelly Sachs captures this shift in perspective in a poem that seems a verbal equivalent of some of Bak's visible intentions:

> Night, night,
> Once you were the bride of mysteries,
> adorned with shadow-lilies—
> In your dark glass glittered
> the illusions of those who yearn
> and love has brought forth its morning rose
> to bloom for you—
> Once you were the oracular mouth
> of dreampainting, mirror of the world to come.
> . . . .
> Night, night,
> Now you have become the graveyard
> for a star's dreadful shipwreck—

time dives speechless into you
with its omen:
The tumbling stone
and the flag of smoke.[5]

Those very omens dominate the paintings in this series. Just as there was an era when remembered pain was only the space between health and hope, so once night was merely an interval between twilight and dawn. But no more. Nature—and humankind—have been immersed in the murky waters of the Holocaust, leaving a residue of spiritual indecision virtually impossible to cleanse. Older rituals of purification are equally stained.

The most mystical—and "difficult"—painting in Bak's series is *Pardes* (fig. 12), an invitation to interpretation that mimics the sages of the Cabbala. *Pardes* is rich in allusion: it is the Hebrew word for orchard, taking us back to the scriptural period of creation; its four consonants in Hebrew (פרדס) represent a devowelized cognate with our word "paradise," with all the ironic overtones carried by that term in a post-Holocaust society; and its individual letters refer to four methods of biblical exegesis—*Peshat* (literal), *Remez* (allegorical), *Derash* (theological or homiletic), and *Sod* (mystical). The painting thus codifies our journey through the "Landscapes of Jewish Experience," with its multiple challenges to the eye and the imagination to consider the impact of the Shoah on traditional forms of worship and belief.

"The alphabet is the land where the spirit settles and the holy name blooms," Nelly Sachs announced in a note to one of her brief dramatic pieces.[6] Bak's *Pardes* draws on a similar recondite conundrum, though with far less certitude. With its downward perspective, the painting reveals two wooden tombs with the tops peeled off in the shape, once more, of the Tablets of the Law. They are divided into two segments, making four in all, each fronted by its own door, each door in turn surmounted by a Hebrew letter: P, R,

12. *Pardes*

D, S. They invite our entry and our interpretation, though the doors close progressively as we move from right to left, emphasizing the difficulty of analysis as time and memory proceed from the simple to the complex, from creation to catastrophe. The last door is nailed shut by two crossed pieces of wood in the shape of an X (another recurrent motif in these canvases), just below the letter S, which signifies the Hebrew word *Sod,* or secret. Enterprising viewers may note that a slight twist of the X to right or left yields a crucifix.

Bak shares with Sachs the belief that meaning must be rebuilt from the ashes of annihilation, saving from the rubble of mass slaughter the murdered word. Sachs called the alphabet "the lost world after every deluge. It must be gathered in," she argued, "by the somnambulists with signs and gestures."[7] And *Pardes* does indeed appear to be a dream landscape, until we accept the imaginative journey through its Kafkalike corridors that carry us from legend to reality—or from nature to cabalistic lore. As we learn to read the signs and gestures of this art, we find ourselves shifting between myth and history and the paradoxes they engender. The Tree of Life in a garden called Paradise had a fellow whose fruit gave birth to death; while the fiery furnace at the end of the voyage, in mystical tradition the origin of the soul, was in our age the greatest source of Jewish havoc known to humanity.

Smoke drifts toward the tree in a meeting of natural forces, leaving us wondering which will prevail. The Jewish narrative of creation moves from chaos to form, from silence to speech and illumination: "Let there be light!" The Jewish narrative of disaster, the story of the Holocaust, migrates from form to chaos, from speech to silence—and the darkness of extinction. The intellectual, philosophical, and artistic landscapes of modern Jewish experience inspire a quest for reconciliation but furnish no guarantee of a successful closure. The problem is that familiar images (like familiar expressions) of consolation cannot cure the wounds inflicted by the loss of European Jewry. A return to the innocence of Eden (or the purity of words) is a futile venture. Sachs captures the dilemma concisely in a few lines:

> But here
> always only letters
> that scratch the eye
> but long since become
> useless wisdom teeth
> remains of a dead age.[8]

As it wanders through the gateways and labyrinths (or scrolls) of the middle zones in *Pardes,* can the imagination rekindle a celestial spark and restore vitality to that dead age? The furnace at the end of the pursuit glows with the holy intensity of divine mystery—but also with the blazing wrath of the consuming flames of Auschwitz.

Does it contain what Nelly Sachs named "the awaited God" or does it contain the demon of mass murder? Are we gazing at an altar—or an oven? Does it invite us to worship—or to die? Are the fragments in its vicinity remnants of sacred vessels—or human skulls? The images before our eyes compel this kind of constant query, as we reenact the need to restore spiritual purpose to a shattered world while discovering through our very search the possible folly of our efforts. The ladders in the painting invite entry and offer escape, matching the inner voyage that divides our choices between peril and hope. If we allow the intricacy of Bak's images to invade our lives, we find ourselves exploring a realm both sinister and benign, a domain of deathlife or birthdeath that requires a new vocabulary such as this, as well as a fresh catalyst for perception.

A favorite term in *Nazideutsch*—a special language devised by the Germans to conceal and express their plans for the Final Solution—was *ausrotten,* to uproot or extirpate, and by association, to exterminate. "Uprooting," of course, is part of the history of the Jewish people, and Bak exploits this dual usage to inspect that experience in past and present. The central motif in *Family Tree* (fig. 13) and *Destinies* (fig. 14) is a tree severed from its trunk or ripped from the earth, but in neither instance has this violation of nature led to its death. Less a miracle of renewal than a stubborn resolve to stay alive, the continued survival of the Jewish people is confirmed in the small shoots that spring from the base of the trees even as the upper trunks are sheared away. Hidden amid the fading golden leaves shaped like Stars of David in *Family Tree* is a rising limb with two vertical branches, a cruciform echo that the murder of the Jews has been a calamity for Christianity, too. The landscape of Jewish experience shares its terrain with its coreligionists, though responsibility for the atrocity is unequally divided. The degree to which the Christian spirit may have been morally tainted by the physical uprooting of the Jews is a muted theme in several of these paintings.

13. *Family Tree*

The basic question is whether the natural principle of growth
that is native to life can be stifled by enemies bent on wrecking it.
In the past, the roots of the children of Israel have shifted between
a fixed and a portable status, and these two paintings capture those
twin options, that have not changed through millennia. In *Family
Tree* the trunk stays anchored to the soil, while in *Destinies* even the

14. *Destinies*

roots have been torn from the earth and seem fated to be transferred to more fertile ground. In *Destinies,* some leaves are fashioned like metallic Stars of David, lifeless and even reminiscent,
with their shieldlike sheen, of the violence that destroyed the people who were forced to wear their originals as emblems of shame.
The amputated trunk is supported by crutches of uncertain origin,

15. *De Profundis*

hardly a happy image of the triumph of survival. Yet the lingering roots have not withered, their remaining vitality yearning for
transplantation, by awaited men if not by Sachs's "awaited God."

Can life be repaired or replenished by animating the erosions of
death? Looming in the foreground of *De Profundis* (fig. 15) are two
vacant gravesites not only shaped like giant Tablets of the Law but
containing their fractured remnants. An arid, Negevlike terrain

stretches into the distance. But the adjacent paintings of trees with roots intact, together with our sense of how parts of the Negev have been cultivated in modern Israel, conspire to remind us of the rhythm of loss and renewal that has allowed Jewish life to be propped up, like the sides of the tombs in *De Profundis*, in the very jaws of extinction. The force of ancient laws may seem to perish, like the splintered letters of the Commandments in this painting, but Bak refuses to seal the crypt and with it all hope for a thriving Jewish existence. Some meager emblems of possibility survive, though as with those who were still alive when the Holocaust drew to a close, there are few occasions to rejoice in Bak's visions and much cause to mourn. A piece of ladder at the painting's edge hints at some chance of flight, while a narrow road winding toward the horizon speaks of a journey still to be taken. But the burden of memory, the personal and ritual loss, dominates the scene, as the broken contents of these mausoleums invite us to consider whether the price we pay for the anguished passage from grave to growth is too high.

Bleakness is a permanent legacy of mass murder, the frame from which all post-Holocaust art must emerge. If most of Bak's landscapes are dreary, however, the fault is history's, not his. One of the many virtues of his work is a resolute refusal to melodramatize or sentimentalize his art. We learn nothing of the "agony" or the "dignity" of dying in these paintings, all but three of which introduce the muted theme of the annihilation of European Jewry through the absence of human figures. Only three contain vestiges of mortality, but even they are associated with art more than with life, and the first and the last, *Self Portrait* and *The Sounds of Silence*, enclose the series with some vital questions about the limits of representing a catastrophe like the Holocaust. Almost midway between the two is *Nuremberg Elegie*, a modern variation on Albrecht Dürer's famous etching *Melencolia I* of 1514, with its somber female figure meditating on the ruins of time—though critics have

16. *Self Portrait*

never agreed on the exact sources of her dismay. But rather than illustrating the anxiety of influence, Dürer's bequest to Bak, the intermediate role of *Melencolia I* suggests the influence of anxiety, the loss of continuity between two artistic visions and traditions, owing to the intervening disruption of an atrocity that Dürer could not have imagined and Bak cannot escape.

Self Portrait (fig. 16) is a portrait of the artist as a young boy, though the child will turn out to be father to the mature man. Among the many crimes committed by the Germans against the Jewish future was the murder of more than a million helpless children. The initial painting in Bak's series is a vivid reminder of the deathlife that is a vexing if paradoxical birthright of that crime: no one's survival can be detached from the loss of someone else.

The boy sits in a sack as if emerging from a cocoon of death, though only those privy to Bak's personal ordeal will be able to grasp the allusion, which seems allegorical but is not. Sent with his son from the Vilna ghetto to a labor camp nearby, Bak's father hid him in a sack, which he then dropped unobserved from a ground-floor window in the warehouse where he was working. Through an arranged plan, the young Bak was met by the maid of a relative who was raised as a Christian and taken to a safe haven. The memory of that moment turns his expression inward in the portrait, making him virtually oblivious to his external environment.

But the viewer is not. Through one of the great ironies of Holocaust history the other child in this picture, a casualty of the Warsaw rather than the Vilna ghetto, immortalized through the best-known photograph to outlast the catastrophe, is far more familiar to us than is the image of the living boy. With his hands raised, fear and confusion in his eyes, he is imprinted on what appears to be the remains of a primitive wood and canvas surface as the archetypal victim, from whose existence the artist-to-be will inherit an important influence on his version of reality. *Self Portrait* thus contains portraits of several selves, including our own, since a central motif of the series to which this painting forms the introduction is the question of how a post-Holocaust era can absorb such a vast atrocity without abandoning the challenges of life or the summons to art.

Primo Levi has written in his memoir of Auschwitz that death begins with the shoes. He meant that a worker whose feet were not properly protected soon lost his or her mobility, hence chance for survival. The pair of empty shoes so prominently displayed in *Self Portrait* awaits an occupant. The boy with his hands raised no longer has need of them, as his feet fade from flesh to painted wood. The feet of the child who was Bak are still hidden in the sack, not yet ready to pursue the arduous journey that will lead from life through death to art. Who indeed is qualified to undertake that voyage? The dazed look on the boy's face betrays only a dim perception of what lies before him.

Unlike the missing slipper that fit Cinderella and turned a scullery maid into a happy princess, these shoes are not the stuff of fairy tales or myth. Are they emblems of the awaited artist, who unlike Nelly Sachs's "awaited God" has the painful task of finding shapes for the chaos of atrocity and thus rescuing it from oblivion? The child-artist is here surrounded by mementos of disaster, not only "The tumbling stone / and the flags of smoke" of the poet's imagination that crowd the edges and corners of the picture, but also the blank pages strewn at his feet that must be filled with the story of a world aflame and a people destroyed. The small stones holding them down commemorate death in Jewish tradition, not creation; yet if "Landscapes of Jewish Experience" heralds anything, it is that the Holocaust has bonded death with creation now and forever, *l'olam va'ed*.

That world aflame hovers not only in the recesses of our mind as we gaze at this painting but also as part of the distant vista. At this point in his career, the boy-artist sees less than his audience, though by the end of the series art will transform our vision and his. Indeed, traces of future paintings tempt us to see *Self Portrait* as a literal prologue to the act of creation. The boy sits on a rocky expanse resembling the uninhabited stone promontory of *Alone,* while across the water the smoking stacks of a vessel foretell the crewless stone ship of *Journey* (fig. 17). And the giant canvas in the upper left corner of this painting, still innocent of any brushstroke, augurs the destiny of the artist himself, who will grow up to create the "Landscapes of Jewish Experience."

But first he must submerge himself in the details of history and the techniques of art, and develop his intensely personal view of how they intersect while honoring both. Imagining precedes imaging: the artist must witness his own life, and that life in its time,

17. *Journey*

before he can merge them in a larger vision reflected by the images of his art. The choice of Dürer's *Melencolia I* as a link—or, rather, a broken link—between past and present is full of dramatic portent. Bak's *Nuremberg Elegie* is a *Melencolia II,* a sequel to the portrait of a winged and angel-like figure musing on the sadness of the world. Late medieval and early Renaissance thought crowded the imagi-

18. *Nuremberg Elegie*

nation with ideas of discovery and progress, but the brooding intelligence could be overwhelmed by the contrast between these possibilities and the misery wrought by the ravages of war, epidemics, and the quest for power, to say nothing of the religious doubts raised by the incursions of science and technology. The duty of the artist to encompass these contradictions can prove to be a burdensome chore. Dürer gathers into his engraving a dense allegorical clutter of technical apparatus that leaves little room for expressions of the natural and spiritual world. The modern mind has minimal difficulty sympathizing with this dilemma. But Bak's *Nuremberg Elegie* (fig. 18) is no simple imitation of its predecessor. The name of the city whose rallies and trials began and ended the reign of the Third Reich did not have for Dürer the sinister ring that it carries for a contemporary ear. The title is a terse reminder of how the Holocaust has changed the resonance of individual words, even proper nouns.

Its elegiac impact has also altered the content of what we mourn, and how. A popular Renaissance theme was the mutability of time, symbolized in Dürer's engraving by the presence of an hourglass. Erwin Panofsky has described the Dürer work as follows: "The winged Melancholia sits in a crouched position in a chilly and lonely spot, not far from the sea, dimly illuminated by the moon. Life in the service of God is here opposed to what may be called life in competition with God; peaceful bliss of divine wisdom, as opposed to the tragic unrest of human creation." But the Holocaust is not a story of the tragic unrest of human creation. It transmutes mutability into annihilation. The atrocity of mass murder has no tragic dimension, its barbaric destructive power temporarily thwarting the basic impulses of the creative urge. Despite its sporadic gloom, the Renaissance mind laid the groundwork for an age of Enlightenment that still inspires the expectations of the democratic world order. Panofsky points out that Dürer's *Melencolia I* is balanced by his serene and reverent *Saint Jerome in His Study,* utterly removed from the radical prospect of an "awaited God."[9] Such repose never enters Bak's post-Holocaust landscape of Jewish experience.

Instead, Dürer's brooding angel is replaced by a morose helmeted soldier, surrounded by the concrete images—hardly allegorical—of the modern disaster. At his feet lie the brightly colored but tattered remains of what once was a rainbow, sign of a renewed covenant and the deluge's end. The failure of that promise is linked to the default of another pledge of divine origin, perhaps Bak's favorite image, the Tablets of the Ten Commandments, which have tumbled from their stable site. They lie like gravestones askew with some numerals still visible, though unlike the number square in Dürer's etching whose columns all add up to thirty-four, Bak's single digits, especially the "6," bear no mystical or magical overtones. The sixth commandment, "Do not murder," has resulted in the slaughter of six million. It is as if the murder of European Jewry has stripped the mystery from existence, leaving only the barren truth of a spiritual wreckage whose import is all too clear. The signs that earlier intensified life by filling it with symbolic meaning crowd the canvas divested of their ancient complexity. Is it any wonder that the artist in the guise of a soldier, offspring of violent conflict, sits sunk in such meditative gloom?

In the place where the Tablets formerly rested stand and lie two meager candles, their wicks barely flaring, rising into petrified plumes of smoke, etched in the stone. One plume points toward the broken wooden arc that once contained the colors of a rainbow; the other aims at the crossbar of a truncated crucifix, backed and topped by a brick chimney. The physical assault on spiritual truth is reinforced by the military garb of the seated human figure as well as by the splintered crucifix, which now resembles a gallows. A Jewish prayer shawl lies draped across the man's knees, while in his hand, like a writing instrument, he holds an unfolded carpenter's rule, as if he were wondering what message to inscribe on this holy relic.

The single images only create the appearance of complexity; they remain separate and unintegrated in a disintegrating world. Yet paradoxically, through the technique of juxtaposition, the artist has achieved an astonishing unity in his organized grouping of fragmentation. Man is no longer a transparent eyeball, as Emerson would make him, reading spiritual meaning into the signs and symbols of nature. As a consequence of mass murder those signs and symbols have grown tainted. To be sure, in Bak's paintings the eye is in constant motion, but as a source rather than a medium for insight. And its main activity is to struggle internally through the brambles of displaced certitudes.

Initially, a chief incentive for both artist and audience was the desire to perceive with visual fidelity the forms of physical and spiritual reality. But Bak has replaced this priority with the need to *re*-perceive. What we see *is* and *is not* what it once was: smoke, flame, candle, star, crucifix, rainbow, and even the number six. The Holocaust has smitten history, memory, language, and art. *Nuremberg Elegie* invites us to ponder this colossal loss; but it also bids us consider what might be reclaimed from the ruin. The great musical requiems are not always mired in sadness but often soar to glory.

In a moment of uncanny prescience, Dürer recorded in his papers a sentiment that might have given birth to the final painting in Samuel Bak's "Landscapes of Jewish Experience": "A boy who practices painting too much may be overcome by melancholy. He should learn to play string instruments and thus be distracted to cheer his blood."[10] Bak's *The Sounds of Silence* (fig. 19) pays unwitting tribute to this measured advice, though its somber mood might curdle the blood even while wishing to cheer it. This last canvas leaves us with an unanswered question, marked by the large X that presides over the scene: Does art finally triumph over atrocity, or does atrocity as we have known it in our time in the end suck art back into its insatiate maw? Is the art of hearing too expensive a luxury, now that our eyes have been stunned by the frightful sights before us?

In this culminating canvas of the "Landscapes of Jewish Experience," Bak grants to music, the purest of the arts, a dubious future. Just as *Nuremberg Elegie* comments on Dürer's *Melencolia I,*

19. *The Sounds of Silence*

so *The Sounds of Silence* seems a grim scrutiny, though in another medium, of Olivier Messiaen's "Quartet for the End of Time," a piece composed and first performed in a POW camp during World War II. With the sky blocked by a gigantic chimney rising beyond the frame of the picture, this string quartet, resembling an enfeebled modern version of the Four Horsemen of the Apocalypse, mimics harmonies muffled by a bizarre acoustics of death. One member is blindfolded, still wearing his striped inmate garb; another is masked; and a third appears to have lost his fleshly contours and is sketched instead on the surface of a block of stone. The cello is blue, the viola discolored, small wonder when we recall the abuse of music in Auschwitz, where some prisoners were forced to play while others were marched to work. The impulse to art has survived its humiliation, but the appeal of the performance, like the diminished worth of the wooden angel's wings shorn of divine vitality, is curtailed by the crumbling remains of a papier-maché ghetto lying at the players' feet.

This is Samuel's Bak's final version of the deathbirth of art. Just as in *Self Portrait* the future of the boy-artist has been certified by the fate of the boy-victim from the Warsaw ghetto, so here the outlook for music, and by extension for all art, is shaped—or, more exactly, distorted—by the rubble of mass murder. But this series has not only concerned the deathbirth of art; equally vital has been the issue of the deathbirth of faith. The history of the Holocaust has dismembered both, art and faith, leaving us with the dual dilemma of retrieving from the ashes of this monumental destruction a phoenix of beauty and a phoenix of belief. Legend and human need coalesce into a new fruition, as the "human form divine" sheds its ancient trappings and redefines its perpetual quest for fresh identity and meaning.

Robert Frost once noted that art comes not from grievances but from grief. Bak begins his series with the personal dimensions of this grief, the loss of the city of his childhood, the Vilna that was the jewel of intellectual, religious, and artistic inquiry in the diadem of eastern European Jewry. He then spreads that grief to include the disgrace and dispersal of the tokens and symbols that lend vigor to the Jewish imagination. In the vestibule of annihilation, the setting for *The Sounds of Silence,* with its looming brick chimney and thin smokestack in the distance, no Star of David shines, no tallow flames from the memorial candle. Perhaps, for Bak himself, the rituals of belief have been replaced by the equally demanding rituals of art. His paintings are his acts of devotion, his tributes to remembrance. At the risk of irreverence, one might argue that the artist as creator is a human reflection of divine intention, filling the void of a blank canvas with forms that populate a living universe of their own. *The Sounds of Silence* taunts the ear with an unheard melody we are forced to invent, one appropriate to the legacy of atrocity that inspired it. And so with the "Landscapes of Jewish Experience": their images haunt the imagination, challenging us through a veil of visual silence to change their mute provocation into the language and the rhythms of an inner speech.

SIX

Two Holocaust Voices
Cynthia Ozick and Art Spiegelman

I
t is scarcely accidental that so few American writers have addressed the theme of the Holocaust with the direct and vivid imaginative command of their European counterparts. Ida Fink, Aharon Appelfeld, Charlotte Delbo, Tadeusz Borowski, and Primo Levi have created classic fictional and nonfictional works unequaled by all but a few of even the most accomplished authors in this country. Of course, Levi and the others had a unique advantage: they could depend on personal memory and experience to conjure up their tales because all of them had been involved as victims of the catastrophe themselves.

The same cannot be said of Cynthia Ozick and Art Spiegelman, although as a child of survivors Spiegelman was able to base his narrative on the ordeal of his parents. Still, both he and Ozick had to face a challenge that their fellow writers from Europe were spared. They had to decide how to imagine this inaccessible event for themselves before they could expect readers to embrace their vision. Indeed, Spiegelman includes this very issue as a major source of tension in his *Maus* volumes. Whether writing biography and autobiography, as Spiegelman does or, as in Ozick's case, trusting pure invention, establishing an authentic voice and persuasive milieu for the uninformed memory of an American public was a critical problem they could not disregard.

The parallels between Ozick's Rosa stories and Spiegelman's *Maus* tales reveal some curious conjunctions. She writes about a mother who has lost her daughter, he about a father who has lost his son. Ozick does everything in her power to detach herself from her protagonist, suppressing the autobiographical impulse by creating a woman who, unlike her, is ashamed and disdainful of her Jewish heritage. Art Spiegelman, in contrast, cannot escape the net of personal family conflict. He is a character in his own narrative, weaving autobiography, biography, and history into a single text. Whereas Ozick harnesses the resources of style to brighten and complicate her fiction, Spiegelman reduces written lines to a minimum, using dialogue as an adjunct to the unique *visual* form he has created to draw readers into the actual world of his father's (and mother's) Holocaust past. Both Ozick and Spiegelman sympathize with the individuals whom they recreate, but they portray them with so many unappealing traits that the reader is both intrigued and repelled by their personalities. Ozick's Rosa and Spiegelman's Vladek continue to be haunted by their Holocaust past. But whereas Ozick carefully conceals her presence through her art, Spiegelman deconstructs his chronicle by constantly reminding us that his version of his parents' ordeal under the Germans is nothing more than that—a version. It is based on testimony rather than imagination, a painfully wrought rendition of reality, not to be confused with the unrecapturable truth.

Because Ozick's Rosa and Spiegelman's Vladek are innocent, victimized by atrocities not of their own making, we instinctively feel pity for them, though their creators are careful to burden them with enough distasteful features to repel readers even as they are attracted. Heroes and heroines belong to romantic legend, not Holocaust reality. Instead of being ennobled by the catastrophe they endured, Rosa and Vladek seem unable to escape its scarring legacy. Ozick and Spiegelman refuse to tell a story of the triumph of the human spirit, the vindication of suffering through transcendence. They know one pays a price for surviving Auschwitz and the other deathcamps; the debt may be suppressed, shifted to a lower level of consciousness, but never forgotten. Closure is impossible: Vladek's ailing heart and Rosa's ailing mind are constant signs that they must share the normal world they inhabit with the abnormal one they inherit.

Unlike Art Spiegelman, whose visual narrative invites us to engage his material on multiple levels, Ozick must rely on verbal ingenuity alone to convey the split milieu in which Rosa dwells. The virtuosity of her technique is dazzling. Language both transfigures and disfigures reality, as contrary descriptions sketch in the competing tensions of her ordeal. In "The Shawl," the story recounting the murder of Rosa's child, Magda, nature is compelling: "the sunheat murmured of another life, of butterflies in summer." But the physical stench of the barracks is revolting: "excrement, thick turd-braids, and the slow stinking maroon waterfall that slunk down from the upper bunks, the stink mixed with a bitter fatty floating smoke that greased Rosa's skin."[1] If there is a branch of art called the poetry of atrocity, this line alone makes Ozick one of its practicing masters.

For Ozick, how we see hinges on how we say, and memory in turn relies on the language of recall to determine how one survives an anguish like Rosa's. The physical fact is that Magda wanders out of the barrack and is seized by an SS man, who hurls her tiny body against the electrified barbed wire. But the moment is imprinted on Rosa's mind by Ozick's stylized portrayal: "The whole of Magda traveled through loftiness. She looked like a butterfly, touching a silver vine." This view is both poetic and remote, since Rosa is not very close to the scene of the murder: "the speck of Magda," we are told, with words verging on the sinister, "was moving more and more into the smoky distance" (9). The opposition between butterfly and smoke will haunt Rosa into her contaminated future, as the fragile beauty of what might have been contends with the reality of what is inside a woman who has outlived her loss but not her pain.

Unlike Vladek Spiegelman, whose financial means allow him to enjoy some of the amenities of American middle-class life, Rosa remains a displaced person even more in the United States than in Europe. She is a fringe being, kept on the outskirts of society by her modest means as well as by what Ozick calls "the drudgery of reminiscence" (69). She violates the stereotype of the immigrant who sheds her burdensome past and finds success in her adopted land. For Ozick, this would have been a formula too easy, too glibly American, to pursue. In her Brooklyn store, where she sells cheap antiques, Rosa tries to tell her customers about the ghetto and the camp, but no one wants to hear. Her complaint is familiar among survivors: "Nobody knew anything" (66). When she moves to Miami, following the path of another kind of Jewish migration, little changes. There, nature pursues her with an ominous intensity: "The streets were a furnace, the sun an executioner" (14). She lives amid Jews, but not among them. Something is missing from her life—is not this the meaning of her "lost" underwear?—and nothing in the American landscape, not laundromats or cafeterias or her cheap hotel, can replace it. At least this is her stubborn conviction.

When Rosa tells the elderly Jew named Persky, a prewar Polish immigrant who tries to befriend her, that "my Warsaw is not your Warsaw," she reminds both him and us that the Holocaust is as misplaced in America as is Rosa herself. But she tells us more, and this is the crux of the tension dominating Ozick's Rosa stories. Rosa allies herself to a Polish professional and intellectual aristocracy rather than to a proud Jewish tradition, and in so doing she forfeits much of the sympathy she has gained from our knowledge of her camp ordeal. She speaks so disparagingly of Jews in the Warsaw ghetto—"we were furious because we had to be billeted with such a class, with these old Jew peasants worn out from their rituals and superstitions" (67)—that she is dangerously close to adopting the prejudice of her German persecutors. American readers are first shocked by her hostility to her own people, then driven to find a middle ground between sympathy and dislike for Ozick's disheveled and eccentric protagonist.

If one purpose of biographical narratives, whether fiction or nonfiction, is to integrate the character of their subjects, then both Ozick and Spiegelman are guilty of subverting this intention. Rosa and Vladek struggle to restore the shattered identities that their German oppressors were determined to efface, but mere chronology cannot erase the deep discontinuities of their lives. Although at the end of her story Rosa removes the shawl from her telephone and, accepting its message, allows the persistent Persky to come up to her room, Magda is not gone, only temporarily away. Rosa's injured maternity has not recovered from the scar etched on her memory by the murder of her daughter. She may give the human instinct another chance, but it cannot cancel the inhuman one that still lingers in the wings of her life's drama.

Unpleasant as she is in her speech and person, bleakly as her anti-Jewish sentiments continue to resound in our ears, the image of Rosa as a bereft mother rescues her from total censure. Vladek Spiegelman's chronic stinginess, his manipulation of his son's and wife's affections, and his outrageous bigotry against blacks make it plain that his camp ordeal—this is true for Rosa, too—has taught him little about generosity toward others. "Learning from experience" in the sense of moral education is a romantic and sentimental stereotype that both Ozick and Spiegelman seem determined to explode. Yet the harrowing narrative of what Vladek and Artie's mother, Anja, endured in ghetto and camps, in hiding and flight, the stories of the murder of family members, including Artie's own brother, can only rouse our sympathy and concern. Like Ozick, Spiegelman draws up two scenarios, forcing us to absorb both, allowing us to be comfortable with neither. Because they coexist in the internal lives of their protagonists, they coexist in ours, too, keeping in permanent tension the flow of chronological time and certain fixed moments of disaster from the past.

One of the recurrent refrains in Charlotte Delbo's Auschwitz memoir, *None of Us Will Return,* is "essayer de regarder, essayer pour voir"—"try to look, try to see." Spiegelman adopts this entreaty as the governing artistic principle of his work. I know of no other Holocaust account that uses it with such literal expertise. Spiegelman takes a familiar artifact of American popular culture, the comic strip, and elevates it to the level of serious literary biography. The visual style of *Maus* enables him to condense both time and space with an economy that is not possible in a prose narrative. On a single page he can move from the United States to Europe, from the city to the country, from Artie's home to his father's. He can alternate closeups with long shots, external with internal views of the same scene, forcing the reader to hold them in suspension while examining the chronicle from multiple perspectives. He can shift time as quickly as he maneuvers space, so that past and present are woven inseparably into one testimonial thread. By showing on the same page an image of Vladek telling his story to Artie, who is preserving his words on a tape recorder, and visual flashbacks recreating the episodes even as Vladek recalls them, Spiegelman can dramatize an ongoing debate between memory and truth. His technique raises a vital question, not only for readers of the *Maus* texts, but for anyone interested in the relation between fictional facts and factual fictions in Holocaust narrative: what changes are wrought by the imagination, even the imagination of the survivor, when his or her history becomes his or her story? What role does the intervention of time play in the effort to portray a past recaptured?

Vladek Spiegelman's testimony is ripe with accurate visual detail. We are not only invited but forced by the pictorial text to imagine features of the Holocaust that often elude even the most diligent reader. We get glimpses of underground bunkers, the inside of a boxcar, roundups, hangings, selections, death marches, the machinery of murder itself via architectural sketches of the gas chambers and crematoria of Auschwitz. The American reader is thus prompted to participate actively in the reconstruction of Holocaust reality emerging from Artie's prodding and his father's reminiscence. Just as Ozick's style tempts us to "see" by what is said, so for Spiegelman the design of a page controls the eye rather than the ear. Historical truth turns visible.

Perhaps the most celebrated example of this strategy at work is the first page of the chapter in *Maus II* called "Auschwitz (Time Flies)." In a succinct fusion of durational and chronological time, Spiegelman shows Artie sitting at his drawing board atop a mound of naked corpses vainly trying to organize the various crucial dates of his narrative and his life into a coherent sequence: the death of his father, the suicide of his mother, the impending birth of his daughter, the murder of Hungarian Jewry in Auschwitz, the enthusiastic critical reception of *Maus I.* Instead of feeling overjoyed by his achievements, however, Artie is depressed.

Why? Like this page, all Holocaust art, whether memoir, biography, or fiction, is built on a mountain of corpses, so that it can never be an act of celebration, a triumph of form over the chaos of experience. "A Survivor's Tale"—the subtitle of both parts of *Maus*—is never entirely that, since in the history of the Holocaust the fact of one person's staying alive cannot be isolated from the death of others less lucky. Indeed, in the Rosa stories and the *Maus* volumes, the impact of dead characters is as great as the role of the living: Rosa's daughter, Magda, Artie's brother, Richieu, his mother, Anja, whose suicide appears to complete the postponed dying she escaped in Auschwitz. Hence Vladek's self-reported ingenuity in manipulating others and devising schemes to keep himself and his wife alive, together with the general fidelity of his testimony, has its darker side.

The elder Spiegelman is not immune to this truth, though he prefers to speak of his more successful exploits. Near the end of *Maus II*, his dejected figure looms down the length of most of a page, photos of his wife's murdered family spread at his feet, while he tells his son of the fate of *his* side of the family: "So only my little brother, Pinek, came out from the war alive . . . from the rest of my family, it's *nothing* left, not even a snapshot."[2] This includes his father, his three sisters with their six children, and three of his brothers. And of course, his own son Richieu.

Because not much of our literature has been erected on a mountain of corpses, or on the prospect of mass murder, American readers are obliged to adapt to an unfamiliar theme. Our greatest classics have been built around memorable names: Natty Bumppo, Hester Prynne, Captain Ahab, Huck Finn, Isabel Archer, Quentin Compson, Willy Loman. Insofar as they are loners, what Melville called Isolatoes, Rosa Lublin and Vladek Spiegelman share their tradition. But unlike their American predecessors, they are not memorable as individuals; they are creatures of an assault on the self that has no parallel in our history—except perhaps for the quite different crime of slavery, or the native American experience, on which Ozick and Spiegelman do not draw in their narratives.

The journey to and from Auschwitz and the other camps injects memory with a poison for which the American cultural landscape provides no antidote. Art Spiegelman confirms this in one of the subtlest touches of the *Maus* stories. Vladek spends one summer in a cottage in the region that used to be known as the Borscht Belt, where wealthy American Jews vacationed in fancy hotels, like the one Vladek sneaks into to play bingo without having to pay. Because the cost of utilities is included in the rent of his cottage, he leaves the flame on his gas burner permanently ignited, so that he won't have to waste matches each time he wants to cook something. We need no Hamlet bitterly crying "Thrift, thrift, Horatio!" to remind us of the sinister echo of this image, a fusion of gas chamber and crematorium that links Vladek inescapably to his dismal past. He may not be conscious of that connection himself, but it exerts its force over his mental life—and ours—nonetheless.

Indeed, how to connect a more or less normal present with a catastrophic past is the theme of both of the texts we have been examining. One role of Holocaust literature is to ease us into a position where we can imagine the struggle for those daily immersed in it. Because it was the story of his life as well as his craft, Art Spiegelman was in a unique position to illuminate that dilemma. He, too, inhabits two scenarios, as Artie the son of Holocaust survivors and Art the artist in quest of a visual narrative form for his experience. He is sensitive to the limitations of his task, admitting in several places the inadequacy of all efforts to reconstruct this atrocity; and to the flaws in his own motives, since he does not even like his father and in fact ignores and exploits his ill-health by smoking in his presence and pushing him to the point of exhaustion with his interviews. The testimony may provide material for Art as well as art, but it brings neither reconciliation nor peace.

I suspect that Ozick and Spiegelman never thought it would, or intended that it should. If one index of American culture is that it offers future opportunities to pacify a painful past, then these American Holocaust narratives challenge us to reshape and deepen that tradition. The opening image of *Maus II* is a photograph of the murdered Spiegelman son and brother, Richieu, to whom the volume is dedicated. But it is also dedicated to Spiegelman's own young daughter Nadja, whose name is not accompanied by a picture. What role will this member of a new generation play in the ongoing saga of her ravaged heritage? Will Nadja be more successful than her father in detaching her existence from the burden of a doomed ancestry?

If the beginning of *Maus II* invokes images of the dead Richieu and the living Nadja, the closing image remains equally ambivalent: the tombstone of Vladek and Anja Spiegelman, countersigned, as it were, by their surviving son, whose signature ends the text, followed by the dates of composition of the *Maus* volumes, 1978–1991. Thus both art and life have a chronology, a beginning and an end. But if the narratives by Ozick and Spiegelman, concerned as they are with an unprecedented event like the Holocaust, mean anything, it is that chronological time is insufficient to contain the impact of its atrocities on human memory and imagination. If life is to go on, we cannot confuse the dead with the living: but this is just what Vladek Spiegelman does in our last glimpse of him on the last page of the book, as he calls his living son by the name of his dead one. Rosa, too, writes letters to her murdered daughter as if she had a real existence beyond her death. Both Ozick's and Spiegelman's narratives are survivors' tales, but we are left wondering in the end who has survived with greater vitality— the living or the dead?

SEVEN

The Stage of Memory
Parents and Children in Holocaust Texts and Testimonies

Among the many human violations visited on victims by Nazi Germany, severing the family bond is one of the gravest. Of course, tales of unwavering devotion abound, and they are justly celebrated. But we are less prone to face those moments when love strove with fear and the need to preserve oneself curtailed the care for others that usually fuses family members into a union of mutual concern. Driven by hardships beyond their imagination, parents and children were often forced to behave in ways that in uneventful times would have seemed inconceivable. As revealed in diaries, testimonies, and memoirs, such moments have left us a legacy of troubled memory that nothing can easily erase.

Consider the following excerpt from the fragment of a young girl's diary in the Lodz ghetto. She remains anonymous, and almost certainly did not survive:

> There is nothing to eat, we are going to die of hunger. My teeth ache and I am very hungry, my left leg is frostbitten. I almost finished all the honey. What have I done, how selfish I am, what are they going to say, what

will they spread on their bread now? . . . My mother looks terrible, a shadow of herself. She works very hard. Whenever I wake up at 12, at 1 in the night, she is bent over the sewing machine, and she gets up at 6 in the morning.

I have no heart or pity, I eat everything I can lay my hands on. Today I had an argument with my father. I insulted and even cursed him. And this was because yesterday I weighed 20 dkg of noodles but this morning took a spoonful for myself. When my father came back at night, he weighed the noodles again. Of course there was less. He started yelling at me. He was right, of course; I had no right to take for myself the few precious dekagrams of noodles Mr. Chairman [that is, Chaim Rumkowski, Elder of the Jews in the Lodz ghetto] gives us. I was upset, and I cursed him. Father just stood at the window and cried like a child. No stranger ever abused him like I did. Everybody was at home. I went to bed quickly without touching supper. I thought I would die of hunger.[1]

This is a far more severe portrait of family tension than the one we get in Anne Frank's universally acclaimed *Diary of a Young Girl*. Here craving for food, not love, is the main motive for conduct; the psychological and spiritual sustenance that Anne received from her father's sympathy is displaced by a gnawing urge for physical nourishment. Starvation is an unholy partner in the quest for survival.

One of the most bitter effects of passages like these is how blame is deflected from the real culprits, the people who have cut off supplies from the Jews in the ghetto, to the victims themselves. A famished person would have to be a saint to resist the temptation faced by this young diarist to eat some of the food before her. The epithet "selfish" with which she charges herself reveals an ideal of integrity that she clings to internally even though her actions betray what she considers a weakness in her physical response. Innocent as she is of the crisis in which she finds herself, the need to detect "guilt" and the absence of an identifiable enemy prompt her to turn first against her father—also entirely innocent—and then against herself.

Misplaced shame and remorse can be so vehement at times that one can be beguiled into endorsing them as valid images of the truth. Among the remnants of writings from the Lodz ghetto is a brief piece called "A Father's Lament," written in Yiddish on the back of some soup kitchen records. The context of this father's self-accusation is the demand of the German authorities in September 1942 that twenty thousand children and old people be "resettled" from the ghetto:

> Yesterday I lost Mookha, my sweet little daughter. I lost her through my own fault, cowardice, stupidity, passivity. I gave her up, defenseless. I deserted her. I left the 5-year-old child, did not save her, and I could have done so easily. I killed her myself because I didn't have the least bit of courage. I have blood on my hands, the guilt is mine because I did nothing to rescue her. The Germans were deporting, it was chaotic, like work round-ups, it was so easy to get away. . . . I walked off with Anya, but I left Mookha behind. Instead of hiding with her in the cellar or in the toilet, I put her in a clothes basket and she gave herself away by crying. . . . I, her father, did not protect her, I deserted her because I feared for my own life—I killed . . . I can't write, I deserve to be punished—I am the one who killed her. What punishment awaits me for killing my own daughter? . . . I am broken, I feel guilty, I am a murderer

and I must atone, because I won't find peace. I killed my
child with my own hands, I killed Mookha, I am a killer,
because how can it be that a father deserts his own child
and runs away? How can he run away and not save his
own child? God, if you are watching, please punish me.[2]

Today, we regard with a bewildering and painful sense of irony this
heartbreaking self-indictment of an innocent man who vilifies
himself with reproaches he should be aiming at his persecutors:
cowardice, stupidity, passivity, killer, murderer, guilt. His plea to
the future for his rebuked honor—"What will I do, how will I
atone for this guilt, how . . . "—falls from the wrong lips, and we
must be wary lest we succumb to the tactic of blaming the victims,
using their own words to support such a misguided venture. The
spirit of loyalty between father and daughter here or parents and
children in general has led many witnesses who outlived the murder of European Jewry to testify in their grief to their own culpabil-
ity. In this instance, if not in others, we are obliged to respond with
the familiar maxim "Tout comprendre, c'est tout pardonner"—
even though for most of our examples, properly understood, there
is nothing to forgive.

In some diary entries, the true criminals disappear so completely from the writer's consciousness that the uninformed reader
seems to have no choice but to charge the victims with responsibility for their own moral collapse. Weakened by hunger, Dawid
Sierakowiak died of tuberculosis in the Lodz ghetto at the age of
nineteen. A year before his death, he recorded a passage that still
makes us wince as we read it today:

Our situation at home is again getting extremely tense
and awful. Father, who for the last two weeks was
relatively peaceful and divided his bread into equal daily
portions, lost his self-control again on Thursday and ate
my entire loaf yesterday and today finished the extra half

kilo of bread he gets from Mother and Nadzia [his sister]. He also stole another 10 dkg. from them when he weighed the bread. . . . Today he went to get the sausage ration and ate over 5 dkg. on the street (Nadzia saw him), so that we were all short-changed. He has also managed to borrow 10 dkg. of bread from Nadzia.

Father bought meat today, and with the liter of whey he got for the whole family, he cooked and guzzled it all up. Now there is nothing left for us, so we'll go to bed without supper. Mother looks like a cadaver, and the worrying is finishing her off.[3]

Who can resist condemning the father in this awful tale of family disintegration? Yet we *must* resist that impulse. How do we escape the danger, then, especially strong for future generations of readers, of misinterpreting the text through ignorance of the context? One of the most perplexing dilemmas of taking or watching Holocaust testimonies, which I have been doing for nearly ten years, is understanding the difficulty so many witnesses have believing that they are without fault for the doom that consumed them and members of their families. Whether we speak of annihilation by gas, disease, starvation, or exhaustion, Nazi Germany frequently conspired to force its victims to participate in their own destruction. With utter contempt for those victims, the murderers knew that the instinct to stay alive would too often take precedence over the moral will to resist, especially when one was faced with the uncommon threats to life of gassing, starvation, or physical exhaustion. The inner struggle between caring father and starving man is an unequal contest to begin with. Unfortunately, when representing such strife, we follow Dawid Sierakowiak in shining a brighter light on the conflicted self than on those who caused the conflict.

My last example of such strife, before turning to Elie Wiesel's contribution to the theme, is from the testimony of a man who outlived the agonizing episode he reports. He describes an *Aktion* in a village in Poland in which he and some other young men are taken to adjacent woods and made to dig a large ditch. They watch as the SS men bring the Jewish villagers by truck to the execution site, line them up at the edge of the pit, and shoot them. Some they kill, others they only wound—but all are thrown, dead or alive, into the mass grave.

Then a moment arrives that leaves us mute, stunned, bereft of response, a scene usually hidden in nightmares or the tales of Edgar Allan Poe, until Nazi Germany enacted it in the real world and turned it into horrifying truth. The witness describes the incident: "They used to throw the earth on the top, and the earth used to go up and down because they are living people. One—the son bury his mother; the mother was still alive [and called out]: 'Moyshe, ikh leb; bagrub mikh nisht lebedikerheyt' [Moyshe, I'm alive, don't bury me while I'm alive]. . . . But Moyshe had no choice, because the Germans [don't] give him the choice. And he bury [her] alive." The interviewer is aghast: "He buried his mother alive?" she asks.[4] The witness shrugs his shoulders and remains impassive. He knows the meaning of what I call "choiceless choice," when a decent human being, though free of blame, is left only with the options of bad or worse. Moyshe might have leaped at the nearest SS man, jumped into the grave himself, refused the task of burying the dead—and the not-yet-dead. But all were sure forms of suicide, and who can indict a living man, even a living son, for flinching from such alternatives?

We do not know the fate of the son; presumably he died, too. Is it cruel of us to add, "At least, we hope so"? Had he survived, what annual ritual would he perform to mourn the death of his mother? One of the harshest legacies for those who outlived such slaughter was that their existence offered them no satisfying gesture of commemoration. Moyshe's mother did not "die"; nor was she "killed," in the ordinary sense of that word. Her murderers, by design, deprived her, like all the others in that mass grave, not only of her life but also of her death. Among the many crimes committed by those murderers is the cutting of the bond that joins a human being's life to his or her death and connects both in turn to the memories of those who will remember them.

This paralysis of memory remains a dilemma for survivors who seek a proper ceremony to commemorate the often unknown end of family members whose flickering life was snuffed out indifferently by their murderers. "The anniversary of the death of a certain Shlomo ben Nissel falls on the eighteenth day of the month of *Shvat,*" Elie Wiesel began his brief essay "The Death of My Father." "This year, as every year since the event, I do not know how to link myself to it."[5] One is reminded of Primo Levi being told by a German guard in Auschwitz, "Hier ist kein warum," when he asked why he could not break off a piece of an icicle to quench his thirst. As Wiesel makes clear in his essay, as well as in *Night* and many other writings, there are no answers to such questions, only questions to such answers. Traditions of parental care did not keep some famished fathers from eating their children's portion of food. Rigorous rules for mourning the dead could not guide Wiesel into a consoling routine for honoring the memory of his father.

Wiesel's description of this breach between the event and our consciousness of it is a prototype for all those victims who fell prey to a world ruled by the ruthless principle of "Hier ist kein warum": "His death did not even belong to him. I do not know to what cause to attribute it, in what book to inscribe it. No link between it and the life he had led. His death, lost among all the rest, had nothing to do with the person he had been. It could just as easily have brushed him in passing and spared him. It took him inadvertently, absent-mindedly. By mistake. Without knowing that it was he; he was robbed of his death" (2). How does this differ from anyone who dies of a sudden illness or accident, deaths as "inadvertent" as the one Wiesel is speaking of? The clue lies in the phrase "lost among all the rest." The one source of identity left to most of us in the closing moments of our life is the so-called dignity of private dying. Family members are left to grieve and to reflect on the "meaning" of the life that is ending or has just abruptly—and sometimes even violently—ended. But Wiesel protests that he is unable to *interpret* his father's death, once more providing a model of response for the thousands of others left in similar situations: "I am ignorant of the essentials: what he felt, what he believed, in that final moment of his hopeless struggle, when his very being was already fading, already withdrawing toward that place where the dead are no longer tormented, where they are permitted at last to rest in peace, or in nothingness—what difference does it make?" (4). In place of a communal ritual of separation, where grief and mutual solace mingle, children and parents faced a sudden disappearance from a barrack bunk in Buchenwald, or the flick of a finger or baton, whose meaning was understood too late by those whose doom it signified and those temporarily spared that doom. The absence of links left one guessing, an eternal doubt about final moments and last intentions, a game of surmise that cannot bring relief.

I am reminded of the closing words of one witness whose testimony lasted more than two hours: "How did my mother look? When did they take her away?" Since such questions remain unanswered and unanswerable, only imagination can fill the void with possibilities, and this is exactly what Wiesel does, changing a victim back into a person, but always with the honest admission that a subtext of silence erodes his text of speech.

Like a painter sketching in various postures for a figure on his canvas, Wiesel creates options for a man who at the end of his life had been denied any:

Through puffy, half-closed eyelids, he looked at me and, at times, I thought with pity. He was leaving, and it pained him to leave me behind, alone, helpless, in a world he had hoped would be different for me, for himself, for all men like him and me.

At other times, my memory rejects this image and goes its own way. I think I recognize the shadow of a smile on his lips: the restrained joy of a father who is leaving with the hope that his son, at least, will remain alive one more minute, one more day, one more week, that perhaps his son will see the liberating angel, the messenger of peace. The certitude of a father that his son will survive him.

In reality, however, I do not hesitate to believe that the truth could be entirely different. In dying, my father looked at me, and in his eyes where night was gathering, there was nothing but animal terror, the demented terror of one who, because he wished to understand too much, no longer understands anything. His gaze fixed on me, empty of meaning (4–5).

A painful game of memory that no player can win: pity, joy, and terror are only as close to or as far from the truth as the imagination will allow. In time, of course, each of those who outlived the catastrophe came to terms with his or her legacy of loss, resumed the text of living and found gestures to continue. But this does not alter the subtext of the narrative, the place where, as Wiesel says, "night was gathering," and still gathers, for those of us who return to its dismal landscape in feeble quest of illumination.

Elie Wiesel's autobiographical memoir *Night* has introduced generations of American readers to that arduous journey, but the light it sheds is more akin to Milton's "darkness visible" than the dazzling brightness of Dante's final vision of the "love that moved the sun and the other stars." In the universe of Auschwitz and Buchenwald, power displaced love as a source of fulfillment. Family members who thought the solace of mutual concern might support them in their ordeal quickly learned how fragile that value would become in their new "home." Although the German masters ruling the camps scorned such loyalties, they could not stifle them entirely, and many survivors I have interviewed attribute their survival in part to the constant presence of a sibling or parent. But such loyalties, as *Night* with its steadfast rejection of sentimentality reminds us, frequently strove in vain against enemies they could not resist with simple human care: German brutality, typhus, exhaustion, dysentery, fear for their own safety, and, perhaps most of all, the utter indifference of their persecutors to their anguish. Such foes drive a wedge between a human being and his or her normal responses or inclinations.

Perhaps the greatest crime of the Holocaust, after the mass murders, is that decent men and women were often forced to violate their natures in order to stay alive. One of the most painfully authentic moments in *Night* occurs when the Kapo Idek beats the elder Wiesel for not working hard enough: "I had watched the whole scene without moving. I kept quiet. In fact I was thinking of how to get farther away so that I would not be hit myself. What is more, any anger I felt at that moment was directed, not against the Kapo, but against my father. I was angry with him, for not knowing how to avoid Idek's outbreak. That is what concentration camp life had made of me."[6] The relentless honesty of the narrative thwarts the impulse to transform this episode into an instance of heroic defiance, though many less scrupulous memoirists have succumbed to that temptation. Wiesel gives us a glimpse into the twisted "morality" that the Germans introduced into the ghettos and camps by depriving their victims of the most elementary source of dignity, the chance to control the results of mutual concern, especially among family members. In this passage, the young narrator shifts the blame from the intermediate culprit, the Kapo, to the victimized father, simultaneously deploring his own behavior while verifying the absence of any meaningful alternatives that might have inspired it. Thus guilt is transferred to the innocent, and the guilty remain unmentioned. The Kapo is an intermediate culprit because the Germans who licensed him to beat prisoners are the original agents of the cruelty. Educated readers know this, but those less informed in the future will have trouble disentangling the features of this perverse morality. Throughout Wiesel's text, the SS are represented by faceless figures and anonymous voices, like the guards who shoot stragglers on the march from Auschwitz to Gleiwitz but are otherwise unidentified.

The paradox of the disappearing criminal grows all the more striking in *Night* as Wiesel describes other father-son relationships. These do not reflect the deeper intimacy between Wiesel and his father that persists throughout the ordeal of Auschwitz. They grasp each other's hands at many junctures, like Adam and Eve in *Paradise Lost* before the expulsion from Eden. The human bond between them may be interrupted, but it is constantly renewed. This is not true for Bela Katz, who tells of putting his own father's body in the crematorium oven; or Rabbi Eliahou, who never learns that he has grown to be too great a burden for his son; or the young boy who beats his father for not making his bed properly; or the father and son locked in fatal combat for a morsel of bread in the open boxcar to Buchenwald. By avoiding a dominant archetypal image of paternal and filial conduct, Wiesel induces the reader to switch moral stances repeatedly, much as the Germans required of the Jews. The individual was left mired in a realm of dwindling choices, deprived of the trustworthy models for virtuous action inherited from a prior life.

The longing to retain the old father-son linkage coexists to the end with the concurrent discovery of its gradual disintegration. The tension between what is emotionally and ethically desirable and what is necessary for physical survival remains one of the central challenging issues for anyone wishing to enter what Primo Levi has called the gray zone of the Holocaust universe. But Wiesel darkens the shading with a brushstroke that is virtually absent from Levi's secular texts. The atrocity of Auschwitz has cracked the solidarity between God the divine Father and his "children," the Jews, leaving a celestial space that remains empty for the young narrator of *Night*—though of course Wiesel's position has evolved from that original point of bleak negation.

Over the years, publishers have continued to include with *Night* the introduction by François Mauriac that appeared in the first French edition, until it seems as if Mauriac's words are a part of the text itself. In an important way, they are, though not as their author intended: in reality, they provide an antitext to the tale that follows. They reflect Mauriac's retreat from the dark intent of Wiesel's narrative, his effort to impose consolation rising from his own needs and belief rather than from the story of the young boy before him. His description of the look on that boy's face, "as of a Lazarus risen from the dead," initiates a myth we have still not escaped from by grafting the language of redemption onto the experience of mass murder and transforming it into nothing more than the universal mystery of human suffering.

If the closing image of *Night* affirms anything, it is that the face in the mirror is a corpse, not a miracle of renewal. Intending no disrespect, Mauriac nonetheless achieves a misunderstanding, one that has unfortunately echoed down the decades, as if the statehood of Israel could ever compensate for the loss of two-thirds of European Jewry. Speaking with the voice of prophecy and wishing to solace, Mauriac verges on insensitivity and certainly diminishes the crime while ignoring the permanent burden of memory when he proclaims: "Zion, however, has risen up again from the crematories and the charnel houses. The Jewish nation has been resurrected from among its thousands of dead" (x).

Mauriac does us a disservice by confusing two narratives. The Christian narrative of Father and Son may lead inevitably to spiritual fulfillment; but the Jewish narrative in *Night* leads only to contradiction and doubt. Wiesel recalls the first Rosh Hashanah or New Year in Auschwitz, where the service—apparently in Buna-Monowitz—ended with a well-known prayer: "Everyone recited the Kaddish over his parents, over his children, over his brothers, and over himself." And what is the result of this traditional ritual of commemoration? That night, writes Wiesel, when they returned to the barrack, "I raised my eyes to look at my father's face leaning over mine, to try to discover a smile or something resembling one upon the aged, dried-up countenance. Nothing. Not the shadow of an expression. Beaten." Then Yom Kippur arrives, the Day of Atonement. Here, if anywhere, renewal reigns in Jewish spiritual life. The episode closes with the words, "In the depths of my heart, a great void" (65, 66).

One of the most vexing discoveries of the prisoners was how often daily existence was governed by the physical circumstances of Auschwitz—disease, exhaustion, beatings, and the omnipresent threat of death in the gas chambers. Unintentionally, one assumes, Mauriac's litany that "all is grace" shifts responsibility from the disappeared criminal to what he calls a "mystery of iniquity" that none of us will ever penetrate. Hoping to provide us with a key to the text of disbelief that rules *Night*, Mauriac gives us a lock instead, barring the reader from confronting the narrative on its own terms. For him, the cry that "God is dead" falls from Nietzsche's lips, but in *Night* the dilemma originates in the gas chambers and crematoria of Auschwitz. The feeling has a parched source that neither Nietzsche nor Lazarus addresses. The lack of analogies—and Mauriac is not alone in seeking these—helps to explain why this particular past remains *unbewältigte,* unmastered, unovercome.

The most celebrated episode in *Night* is the hanging of the three inmates—two adults and one child. The obvious parallel is the least relevant one, except insofar as the incident reminds us of the failure of Mauriac's faith to forestall or explain the disaster. At this moment, the theme of parents and children divides. The death of a parent is terrible, but the inmates have grown familiar with such scenes. The agony of the child on the gallows, by contrast, recalls one of the first images to greet the young Eliezer upon his arrival in Auschwitz: the burning of babies in a pit of flames. The murder of children emerges in *Night* as the supreme crime of the Holocaust, the act that erodes faith, or at least suspends it on the gallows together with the victims. Iniquity is no mystery here; its agents, the SS, are in plain view. But this is no solace for the children who were turned into corpses. Nor is it any consolation for the surviving boy Eliezer, who in telling his story learns that he must share his future with the memory of the corpse that greets him in the mirror at the end of his ordeal.

This is a dismal conclusion—but not a nihilistic one. The heritage of corpses leads to what I call a tainted memory—not to permanent despair. Parents and children survived Auschwitz and proceeded with their lives. Not with the old ones, of course, but meaningful ones nonetheless. Yet for many of those who outlived the catastrophe, the idea of the family, of parents and children, continues to exist within the shadows of night, a legacy they cannot escape. No reader of Art Spiegelman's *Maus* can fail to note the bitter irony of the final moment when Vladek confuses his living son with his dead one. Anyone familiar with Holocaust testimonies will know that this is not merely a piece of artistic contrivance designed to have a dramatic impact on the reader. It reflects a genuine crisis of identity for Artie, the child of a survivor whose other child was a victim. I remember interviewing one witness who told how her daughter was saddened and confused while growing up when her husband, also a survivor, frequently called their present daughter by the name of his child from a previous marriage who was murdered during the Holocaust. The bond between parents and children in such families, and in thousands of others like them that may not share this particular grief but have other losses to mourn, is an intricate one. Our best tribute to all of them is to try to imagine the role the stress of absence plays on the stage of their memories—a never-ending struggle to reclaim some fragment of those missing lives.

EIGHT

The Inner Life of the Kovno Ghetto

Amajor temptation facing anyone trying to enter the unfamiliar milieu of the Kovno ghetto under German rule is to view it through the lens of values that govern our daily lives. Even though everyone doesn't always follow them, normal society has clear-cut rules about what comprises acceptable and unacceptable behavior: honesty is preferable to lying, sharing is better than greed, and theft violates both law and the principles of decent behavior. But the ordeal of the Jews in the Kovno ghetto did not reflect "normal society," so any effort to ease our discomfort by supporting it with the props of our less threatened existence is bound to distort the truth of their situation. We need to imagine a community whose members were hungry, exhausted, plagued by memories of the murder of friends and family, and haunted by the possibility of a similar fate for themselves.

In the ghetto, smuggling, stealing from, and lying to the Germans became necessary strategies for remaining alive, as human beings struggled to stay afloat amid the twin currents of hope and despair. The atmosphere resembled what Primo Levi called a "gray zone," that uncertain moral realm where a flexible behavior was shaped more by external circumstance than by inner conviction. Neither hope nor despair reigned for long, because ghetto residents could not control their lives in any meaningful way. Although fewer than 10 percent of its inhabitants outlived the disaster of the Kovno ghetto, the voices of those who survived help us to gain a sense of the diverse and often contradictory attitudes that prevailed there. Any effort to assemble a consensus, however, must be doomed from the start.

Unfortunately, no reassuring vocabulary emerges to describe life in a ghetto ringed by the threat of death. Many commentators speak of a "relatively quiet period" of nearly two years in the Kovno ghetto, following the initial slaughter by Lithuanians and Germans after the invasion of the Soviet Union in June 1941. But we should not be beguiled, as some Jews desperately seeking solace may have been at the time, by this interlude in the unrelenting process of mass murder. Today, it is difficult to imagine how anyone who experienced the "great action" of October 28, 1941, when nearly ten thousand Jews were selected to be killed at the Ninth Fort the next day, could erase from memory the unsettling legacy of that event. There was hardly anyone who did not lose a relative to that explosion of violence. Immediately afterward, we are told, "a deep mourning descended on the Ghetto. In every house there were now empty rooms, unoccupied beds, and the belongings of those who had not returned from the selection. One-third of the Ghetto population had been cut down. The sick people who had remained in their homes in the morning had all disappeared. They had been transferred to the Ninth Fort during the day."[1] To assume that mere time could ease the pain of this ordeal is to misjudge the power of such atrocity to capsize the tranquil vessel of the mind. As one survivor of the Kovno ghetto reported many years later, "It stays for you, till today. You never forget it. You dream about it. You can't sleep. You are nervous like a dog."[2]

Ghetto inhabitants thus faced the constant problem of searching for equilibrium by balancing loss against gain, but they did not always solve it successfully. For example, after the Germans burned down the hospital for infectious diseases with patients, doctors, and nurses still inside, what ghetto occupant could ever again believe that he or she was safe from the cruelty of such a regime? Yet the head of the Council of Elders, Dr. Elchanan Elkes, repeatedly sought pledges from German officials that the most recent "action" would be the last one and that the future was relatively secure for the remaining Jews provided they worked diligently and did not openly violate current German laws. In so doing, he expressed a common psychological desire for inner assurance that most human beings depend on in moments of stress. A decent and intelligent man with no interest in advancing his personal needs before those of the community, Elkes could not repress the impulse to seek in his oppressors some faint ember of the honor that warmed *his* life. Today we may deem this a fatal error, but at the time Elkes's behavior only proved how impossible it was for the human consciousness, Jewish or otherwise, to accept as a nonnegotiable finality the doom of an entire people. Hampered by an inadequate knowledge of German intention—a limitation that would have been shared by any other leader in his place—he strove to hold back a flood with a finger in a dike that was bound to collapse eventually in spite of his strenuous efforts.

In his *Kovno Ghetto Diary,* Avraham Tory relates that when the news spread on October 27, 1941, of an order for all Jews in the ghetto to assemble the following morning in Demokratu Square, panic mounted among the residents. Roll calls of such magnitude raised a strong possibility of large-scale selections and mass executions. To allay his people's anxiety, Dr. Elkes asked for a meeting with Sergeant Rauca, at which he "pleaded with 'Mr. Master Sergeant' to reveal the whole truth behind the rollcall." Today we may regard with wonder and dismay the guileless assumption that a Gestapo official would be moved by an appeal to his honesty from a Jew, an appeal based on the belief that beneath the surface of German contempt lay a bedrock of integrity still joining one human being to another. How else can we explain Elkes's language, as recorded by Tory: "Dr. Elkes attempted to appeal to the 'conscience' of the Gestapo officer, hinting casually that every war, including the present one, was bound to end sooner or later, and that if Rauca would answer his questions openly, without concealing anything, the Jews would know how to repay him."[3] Addressing the conscience of a Gestapo official or offering him a kind of postwar "bribe" of support may seem like an absurd idea today (especially when we reflect that in October 1941 the German juggernaut throughout Europe seemed invincible); but a far more complex issue at the time was finding a strategy for facing the crisis without abandoning to total disaster the people whose leadership Elkes had reluctantly accepted.

Tory considered Dr. Elkes's conversation with Rauca a daring maneuver; others might call it foolish or naive. Trust may be a laudable virtue in ordinary times, but when the threat is mass murder, it proves a vulnerable defense indeed. This was certainly the opinion of some other survivors of the Kovno ghetto like Dr. Lazar Goldstein, who spoke of the Germans' use of a Council of Elders as a plan to "rake hot coals with Jewish hands." His view cannot be dismissed simply as mere retroactive resentment. His charge that "step by step the Elders Council became more and more involved in helping Nazis, even if unwittingly, to carry out their diabolical plans," must be addressed.[4]

Large ghettos like Kovno had a public life and a private life, and unfortunately the interests of the two did not always coincide. For example, in their capacity as "public" officials, members of the Jewish Council of Elders had to assign individual Jews to different work squads, some of them, like the airport brigade, requiring exhausting daily labor after a long march from the site of the ghetto. It was natural for some individuals to resent the decisions of the council, seeing in its cooperation a form of collaboration. But in order to prevent the swift and chaotic dissolution of the community, someone had to take responsibility for finding and assigning living space, distributing food, organizing work details, meeting sanitary and medical needs, and handling the dozens of other matters that would make day-to-day subsistence minimally possible. The *intention* of those who finally agreed to accept custody of the ghetto's welfare under the constraints of the German occupation was to wrest some control of the community's fate from a seemingly hopeless situation. This proved at first to be a herculean task and finally, because of the ruthless German determination to destroy all of Kovno Jewry, to be an insuperable one.

In normal times, public life is designed to bolster private expectations, but in the Kovno ghetto so often did one prove an obstacle to the other that a seamless interaction between the two became impossible. On February 4, 1943, immediately after their defeat at Stalingrad, almost as a petty and spiteful act of revenge for their humiliating loss, the Germans rounded up twenty-seven ghetto inmates and sent them to the Ninth Fort for execution. This was in the middle of the period of so-called relative calm between the initial executions and the final liquidation. The effect, Tory says, was a temporary paralysis of Jewish existence at every level: "There was no work at the Jewish institutions in the Ghetto. It was simply not possible to conduct any public activity under the conditions of the prevailing mood of depression. The life of no person is secure any longer. Anyone may stumble all of a sudden. All the same, our will to go on living is as strong as ever—to go on living and to leave the horrors behind."[5] Tory's concluding words in this passage sound paradoxical, since depression rarely coexists with hope. Yet precisely this paradox characterized much of Jewish life during the ordeal of the ghetto, not as a form of denial, but as a desperate effort to ignite amid the gloom of daily despair some spark that might enable the individual and the community to go on.

Today we realize what the Jews of Kovno should have known from the first moment of the ghetto's creation, and from the mass executions preceding it—that, as Tory admitted, the life of no person was secure any more. But such a perception at the time must have been psychologically and emotionally intolerable. Ironically, though the Germans despised the Jews as a species incapable of moral vision, they exploited both the private and the public need to believe in a bond between diligence and endurance, survival and hope. They took advantage of Dr. Elkes's devotion to the idea of a common human allegiance to truth, just as they cynically abused each inmate's desperate faith (and perhaps relief, terrible as it may sound) that if some Jews were expendable to the Germans, others were not.

Even more difficult for us to understand today is the impact of the brutal principle of "collective responsibility" that the Germans imposed on the ghetto residents. This perversion of the idea of moral conduct left the Jews deprived of a sound basis for ethical behavior. As reported by Tory, the Gestapo issued the following order: "labor brigade leaders would be answerable for unauthorized trading and absenteeism from the place of work. If anyone is caught committing these offenses, his brigade leader and the members of his family will be arrested and executed. In more serious cases, several labor brigade leaders will be executed, together with their families. The guiding principle behind this order is: all are responsible for everyone and everyone responsible for all."[6] Ironically, a similar sentiment in Dostoyevsky's fiction makes each man an indispensable partner to the spiritual life of all others; the Germans twisted this principle to make each Jew in the Kovno ghetto a potential indirect accomplice to the physical murder of any other member of the community.

In spite of the German edict, ghetto inhabitants "lucky" enough to work in brigades within the precincts of Kovno city itself continued to trade their remaining possessions with Lithuanians for food in order to keep themselves and their families alive. According to Leib Garfunkel, vice-chairman of the Council of Elders,

"Hunger was one of the severest problems that faced the Kovno Ghetto. It was impossible to survive on the daily food rations that the Germans gave to the Ghetto residents. In actuality, these were starvation rations. The rations given to the Jews represented one-third of the minimum calories required for daily survival."[7] Avoiding death and courting death thus became simultaneous rules of personal existence, though after the German edict the perimeters of risk expanded to include the lives of others. The psychological effect of this tension on those who continued the smuggling we can only surmise, but it must have been overwhelming. Tory himself sees it as a deliberate consequence of German malevolence, though he will not allow even this extreme form of malice to dampen his spirits.

His comments betray the irrepressible human instinct to see some light even in the blackest tunnels, as he mingles his private vision of hope with an acknowledgment of the life of desperate confusion that the Jews' oppressors forced them to lead. He begins with a clear-sighted statement of German intentions: "This is always the way with the Germans. They do not tell you things clearly, except when they curse you and scream at you. It is therefore imperative to assess their mood properly before they open their mouths. We must understand that, from their point of view, our situation must always remain unclear. . . . We are to remain always in a state of anticipation, without understanding what is going on around us." But he follows this with a counter-view that gives us a glimpse into how a strangulating people managed to go on breathing: "However, it is impossible for us to live in a state of permanent nervous tension. Despite the eleven chambers of hell that the Jews—as individuals and as a community—have gone through, our spirit has not been crushed. Our eyes are wide open and we are attuned to what is going on around us. We do not forget for one moment the hallowed purposes of our people."[8] Other commentators would greet with dismay Tory's conviction that "our eyes are wide open and we are attuned to what is going on around us." What was going on around them by 1943 was the unhallowed purposes of the Germans to destroy not only Lithuanian but all of European Jewry, and the members of the Council of Elders were decidedly *not* attuned to this reality.

Indeed, survivors like Dr. Lazar Goldstein argued that rhetoric from council members about keeping the spirit from being crushed *blinded* them to the true nature of German intentions from the beginning. He criticized the members of the Council of Elders for cooperating with Nazi authorities in the "mistaken belief that in this way they would be able to *help* Jews," and even suggested that Dr. Elkes's basic decency made him the *wrong* man to "have been in a position of leadership in such a terribly cruel and critical time."[9] He may have been correct; but who would have been the "right" man, and how was he to be recognized, not to say recruited? Chaim Rumkowski in Lodz and Jacob Gens in Vilna fared no better: these council heads may have been instrumental in postponing the liquidation of their ghetto communities, but not in preventing it. Who knows what qualities of mind or character were necessary to anticipate the German plan to murder all the Jews of Europe, and given that power of insight, what strategies were adequate to greet this gruesome design?

In the absence of a cogent answer—though there is much to deplore in the limited foresight of those responsible for guiding the Kovno ghetto through its hopeless years, and much to admire in the tenacity with which these leaders tried to make the best of an impossible situation—we must conclude that all policies would have led to the same finale, some sooner, some later. A few concessions to special pleading, like temporarily increasing the allotment of food or firewood, fooled the leadership into believing that their powers of persuasion had some impact on the more "reasonable" German minds; in fact, in the end, they could do nothing to halt the doom of the Kovno ghetto.

Many individual Jews in the ghetto had a clearer sense of their ordeal than did their leaders, though for most of them this made little difference after the Germans had decided to kill them all. One survivor wrote later of the period of "relative calm" in the ghetto: "For us normal meant the absence of mass executions or deportations. It meant having just enough food to exist. . . . It meant survival of the community while individuals were shot. It meant life behind barbed wires, like criminals, like slave laborers without rest or relaxation. This was normal in the ghetto."[10] This is much bleaker than the view we get from Tory, who, in addition to the surges of optimism that seemed native to his temperament, as a public official was excused from slave labor, had greater access to food, and was free to leave the ghetto for the city several times weekly. That is why we need to weigh various voices before we reach even tentative conclusions about life in the ghetto before its liquidation.

Although there were resistance groups in the Kovno ghetto (supported by both the Jewish police and the Council of Elders), they were neither numerous enough nor sufficiently armed to mount any meaningful opposition to the Germans. Toward the end of the ghetto's existence, some units of young Jews tried to escape to the forests to join with partisans, but most of them were caught and killed.[11] Resistance was not uppermost in the mind of the average ghetto inhabitant, and one witness who spent three years there offers a possible explanation why. His testimony also sheds light on both the public and private impact of the constant German endeavor to deceive:

> There was always the little carrot that the Germans did, saying, "Now this is the last action. You don't have to be afraid to go to work," saying, "Now, you see, nothing's going to happen to you anymore, because this is the last time." . . . And of course that was all nonsense. Psychologically, of course, we were very glad to be

fooled. If maybe they would be very blunt, it would be a natural reaction to fight, but this way we were just lured into . . . even though we knew that this was not so. But still everybody figured maybe . . . maybe they're telling the truth.[12]

Few analyses capture so succinctly the inner consciousness of a trapped community, its members' will to action paralyzed by simultaneously affirming and denying their utter vulnerability at the hands of the Germans.

Some have celebrated the fact that in Kovno (as in Vilna) concerts and other forms of cultural activity sustained the spirit of the physically oppressed Jews, but here, too, there is no unanimity. Just as in Vilna the librarian Hermann Kruk protested with the famous slogan "No theater in a cemetery," so in Kovno, as one survivor writes, comparing the concert he attended with earlier times, "Most of the people were hungry, tired from slave labor, and the mood was subdued. Everybody had the same feeling: was it really right to have a concert, when the blood of our murdered people was still warm?"[13] One thing is clear to anyone who listens patiently to the voices of those who outlived the catastrophe of the Holocaust. For every "yes" there was a "no," just as here whatever pleasure one derived from listening to familiar music was shadowed if not contaminated by an aura of pain and loss. This does not negate the role of positive feelings in the midst of despair; but it complicates them, and certainly limits the strength of their appeal. When Avraham Tory applauds "the will of our people to live under any conditions and situations," he does so by temporarily suppressing any mention of the oppressive details of those conditions and situations.[14]

For a survivor much younger than Tory, those "conditions and situations" could blight the hope for a brighter future. Tamar Lazerson kept a diary in the ghetto for more than four years, beginning when she was almost thirteen and ending after her seventeenth birthday. The earliest notebooks are lost, but the remaining ones offer a remarkably mature portrait of ghetto existence from the pen of one of the youngest survivors of the ordeal. Not yet fifteen, she describes the end of a working day: "Splashed with mud, trampled with puddles, the curses, sighs of weakened creatures. At long last the gate, the Ghetto. Here is the house! It appears, happiness, but no! Because tomorrow the same trip. One day is identical to the next as two drops of water. A day of black labor, a day of wretchedness . . . and the same outcry for bread, for light. All around is just hunger and darkness."[15]

We delude ourselves if we believe we can enter into the daily existence of the Kovno ghetto without first confronting the physical reality of melancholy visions like this one. Both of Tamar's parents were killed, and after her liberation she described herself in her diary as "a lonely orphan in the world, like a stone."[16] Views like hers may not be the whole truth, but they are the basis on which all other reconstructions must build. If the resultant edifice is morally and spiritually precarious, this is only a testament to the brutal legacy that ended the lives of more than 90 percent of Lithuanian Jewry. Those who survived, like Tamar Lazerson, may have resolved to create for themselves a brighter future, but this does not mean that either they or we could ever escape entirely from the memory of their darker past.

NINE

Undzere Kinder
A Yiddish Film from Poland

The last Yiddish film to be produced in Poland after World War II, *Undzere Kinder* is full of contrasts and contradictions: past and present, daylight and nighttime, memories and expectations, stage drama and real events, heroes and victims, grief and hope, comic distractions and tragic loss.[1] In its structure, the film veers from one term of each pair to the other, though viewers are enjoined to see them not as alternatives or chronological sequences so much as coexisting tensions that never cancel each other out. The children's laughter and play that greet the morning at the film's end do not and cannot dispel the nightmares of the evening before, though they temporarily displace them.

The actors' final tribute to the children—"Thank you, especially for restoring our faith. These children will be far more fortunate than their parents. They can expect a bright future"—will console only those of us who have not been paying attention to the dual rhythm that governs every moment of the film. Shall we say, too, of the surviving mother whose child has been murdered in the ghetto: "This *mother* will be far more fortunate than her child. *She* can expect a bright future"? Only the momentary amnesia of the day can justify such sentiments; but when darkness restores memories of German atrocities, the gloom of recollection reveals how shallow and flawed, how utterly incomplete, is this soothing rhetoric of hope.

Images and formulas for facing the ordeal of the Holocaust abound in the film, beginning with Nathan Rapoport's massive sculptured tribute to the fighters of the Warsaw ghetto: "This monument," we read, "is a testament to their sacrifice and final victory." Propaganda, or truth? Subsequent flashbacks baring the fate of *other* victims make us wonder about the value of an expression like "final victory," to say nothing of a vaguely theological term like "sacrifice." The film, in other words, sabotages the very principles it seeks to establish, forcing us to question the legitimacy of any effort to capture in language or image the inner dimensions of the catastrophe. First we are told that we must "forget our grief and build a new life," but then we are cautioned "never to forget our tragic experience." *Yidn viln fargesn* thus rivals *Yidn kenen nit fargesn* in a polar conflict that continues throughout the film. By day, *we* seem to triumph over the Holocaust; but at night, *it* seems to triumph over us. The cinematic art of *Undzere Kinder* seeks to resolve the dilemma but may merely magnify it.

By questioning the credibility of its own vision, the film offers us one of our earliest examples of the postmodernist tendency to suspect the authority of any narrative voice or form. An early episode presents a sentimental skit about the ghetto experience by two Jewish musical comedy stars who have spent the war years in the Soviet Union and thus have no personal knowledge of what existence was like under the Nazi regime. Their song is designed not to reflect historical truth but to entertain. This proves to be too much for an orphan in the audience, who disrupts the performance by whistling from the balcony because he knows that ghetto reality did not include begging for chicken legs and challah. In their professional search for original material, the actors neglect a basic premise of Holocaust art, which limits the freedom of invention by making a clear distinction between fictional facts and factual fictions. Instead of admitting recent Jewish history into their repertoire, the actors turn to ancient Jewish traditions about mama's home cooking for the lyrics of their ghetto song. Moved by nostalgia rather than a yearning for facts, the listeners in the theater applaud lines like "All will be well and we'll say Amen," since such lines allow them to dismiss the ruin that the Holocaust has wrought upon the Jews of Poland.

The children know otherwise, substituting in their own spontaneous performance in the actors' dressing room "a shtikele broyt" and a cold potato for a slice of goose and a piece of cake. These orphans have lost more than their parents; they have lost the legendary world of Sholem Aleichem, who could sustain his vision of comic pathos amid the intermittent threats of pogrom violence but knew nothing of the brutal finality of starvation and genocide. The actors' version of Sholem Aleichem's "Kasrilevke brent"— which is introduced to us as "a bit of the old Jewish way of life"—is a source of humor, a tribute to their versatile talents, but who can quell the sinister echoes of those other, less quenchable flames that consumed a people? As one of the orphanage workers mutters about their earlier portrayal of ghetto songs, "This is a theme to lament, not to play." Then she complicates her protest by adding, "Silence won't bring us joy either."

The film thus continues to question its own premises, inviting us to reconstrue its conclusions even as it seems to assert them. Chronological time governs one rhythm of the film, as the present tries to escape its past and gain a foothold on the future. If the survivors can learn to "use tragedy creatively," they may subdue their fearful heritage and get on with their lives. But the countertheme intrudes repeatedly, as durational moments of horror from the past surface to remind us and them that atrocity and tragedy may not be the same: artistic and historical models vie for control of our imaginations. Tragedy may indeed be used creatively as a literary form; but the memory of Holocaust destruction lacks a nurturing fervor. The director of the orphanage recalls the frightened cry of her doomed child, but it does not sound like the cooing of two white doves. The actor who sings that song may console himself, but does little to alleviate her pain.

The actors begin—and it is not clear that they ever change this opinion—with a simple-minded view of art as a form of therapy and of the children as "patients" who simply need to be cured of their bad memories. Having spent the war in the Soviet Union—one orphanage employee mentions that they were with the partisans in the forest—they have little idea of the ordeals the children endured. Like the rest of us, they are spectators to the hermetic cruelties of the Holocaust. So like the rest of us, they have their *own* welfare, not only that of the survivors, to consider. They visit the orphanage with little enthusiasm, not in quest of historical truth, but hoping to acquire what one of them calls "wonderful material": the children are "an original source" for their own art. How *do* outsiders approach a reality like the Holocaust, that may be imagined but never "known" except by those who experienced it? The breach gives birth more often to heroic myth than melancholy insight, as Nathan Rapoport's monument confirms at the outset of the film.

Indeed, the seeds of myth frame the film, which begins and ends with the stirring refrain from the famed Partisan Song, "Zog nit keynmol" (Never say this is your last journey), a resolute refusal to accept physical or spiritual extinction at the hands of the Nazis. It reflects a small part of Holocaust reality, but its affirmations must be measured against the grimmer stories told by the children about victims who had no choice in controlling their fate. Like the actors, the partisans are not part of but apart from the anguish of the boy whose mother is shot down and dies believing that her son, too, has been murdered in his attempt to escape. No heroic melodies can diminish the boy's grief. Similarly, the story of another mother's woe who works in the children's home shares the visual setting with a wall photograph of the celebrated figure of Janusz Korczak, head of the Warsaw ghetto orphanage and obviously patron saint to the one in this film. Myths still swirl about Korczak's courageous exploits in caring for his children, though some have called him naive. He, too, had encouraged his wards to use tragedy creatively by urging them to perform plays, such as Rabindranath Tagore's *The Post Office,* about the death of children. But he was still unable to prevent the deportation of all his charges to Treblinka, where they were murdered on arrival, and one is left wondering how their dramatic efforts in the ghetto could have prepared them for such an unimaginable doom.

The question that looms largest in the film is whether the tactics used by those who would represent the events of the catastrophe are anything more than a strategy of diversion, whose deepest if unexpressed aim is to avoid more undigestible details. The actors and their hostesses wish each other "a gute Nakht" before they retire, but "a shlekhte Nakht" is what really lies before the actors, as they wander through the shadowy corridors of the orphanage in search of their place of repose, like Kafka's Joseph K. haunting the halls of the law courts in vain pursuit of justice. Their nocturnal education prompts them to confess, "We came to collect material and instead opened up old wounds," though their impugning of motives is so succinct that we are unsure whether the avowal embraces confusion, remorse, or insight. They draw closer to a threatening truth with the discovery that "this is not a house of children, it's a house of nightmares." Only slowly do we realize that the designation itself is a form of avoidance, since we are speaking of real memories, not the distortions of nightmares. An SS man's cynical barter to Polish peasants of a little girl from a truckload of doomed Jewish children is only too vivid an example of the daytime horrors that the victims had to face, though in the telling it may *sound* like the surreal product of nocturnal imagining. The aged couple who pay for the girl manage to save her life, but with a fearful and hesitant gesture, not a brave act of defiance. How can we limit ourselves to rejoicing at her salvation when she is humiliatingly discarded by the Germans as a piece of worthless trash? If the actors ever do learn to use such "material" for their art, they must first "unlearn" the literary legacies of a Sholem Aleichem, which do not train one to confront the agonies of Holocaust atrocity.

As it turns out, few in the film are willing to surrender so much, including some of the former victims themselves. The orphanage head, who has her own loss to live with, is reluctant to concede that the Holocaust may have inscribed a permanent scar on the memory of survivor and nonsurvivor alike. "If we don't deal with these memories during the day," she argues, "they will suffer them at night as terrible nightmares." This is sound practical advice, but presumably they have been doing just that since the end of the war, and as the film insists, the children still retain vivid recollections of the atrocities that severed them from their parents and fellow Jews, just as she has engraved on her mind the moment when her daughter was taken from her. The film is remarkably prophetic in its formula for the best way of "dealing with" the potentially disabling memories of the Holocaust: picking up the introductory theme of the Rapoport monument and the Partisan Song, one well-intentioned spokesman concludes that they have to "help the children understand how Jews finally resisted and fought." Anticipating both the driving force behind the Heroes and Martyrs Remembrance Authority of Yad Vashem and the Warsaw Ghetto Fighters House at Beit Lochamei haGetaot, this psychological motif continues to reign in some circles as the only balm to soothe the aching wound of mass murder that still mutilates Jewish memory. In order to salvage a present and make a future more possible we need to reshape the past, imposing on history a design that may not have been there during the event but seems, upon reflection, to be a usable way of viewing it.

Thus the film offers us a variety of options for facing the disaster: we can use tragedy creatively as the actors try to do, searching eagerly for new material to feed their routines; or we can use history creatively, molding defeat into victory, the death of the body into the triumph of the spirit, simply by skirting the agony of annihilation and focusing instead on narratives of resistance. To this day, nearly fifty years after the film was made, the story of the Warsaw ghetto uprising and the Partisan Song remain standard icons of memory to transform the anguish of mass murder into a heroic ordeal.

Our responses to these options are tested to the very last moments of the film. The actors finally fall into a fitful and troubled sleep, depressed and overwhelmed by the children's stories that they have overheard. When they awaken, they are eager to depart at once from this Holocaust haunted house. But when they open the curtains, daylight floods their room and the mood abruptly shifts: the children are playing in the sunshine, seemingly untroubled by their nighttime memories. They have returned to chronological time, causing the actors to conclude: "Morning proved that the children are healthier than we are. We have much to learn from them." But they fail to tell us what, leaving us to speculate about the ambiguity of this observation. The concept of "health," so crucial to the medical and psychiatric professions, may not be appropriate to describe the physical or mental status of children who have survived the Holocaust. Indeed, the film has earlier alerted us to a parallel problem for their elders: "The adults are just like the orphaned children—many with spiritual wounds and complexes." The mistake the film *invites* us to make is to assume that the actors have achieved some insight as a result of their visit, but this remains inconclusive to the end. By critiquing its own invitations, the film initiates a dilemma in Holocaust commentary that we are still seized by.

How and what do we "learn" from the survival experience?

Peering from their bedroom window, the actors see the children playing at their own version of "Kasrilevke brent," and the actors conclude that they are making fun of them. This may be true: but does it also mean that they have learned how to use *tragedy* creatively, or merely Sholem Aleichem? And is the subject of their parody and imitation only the actors, or Sholem Aleichem, too? Can children of the Holocaust remain children of the Jewish worldview of Sholem Aleichem? Has there been a rupture in continuity, and do efforts to repair it represent a falsification of experience, especially recent Jewish experience? "Thank you . . . for restoring our faith," the actors smile—but they never say faith in what, so that many of our questions remain unanswered, *unless* we are content to embrace the amnesia of the film's ending, which makes us feel as if the Holocaust never happened or that its impact has shriveled in the heat of the heartwarming sun. As far as the children's "bright future" is concerned, it seems now unstained by the events of their dismal past. At least this is what the relieved actors prefer to assume.

"Zay gezunt, un farges nit di Kinder" (Be healthy, and don't forget the children)—these are virtually the last words spoken in the film, and they join for the final time the issues of health and memory that have threaded through its dialogue and imagery. Remembering alludes not only to the children's present and potential future but also to their past, and their recollections of it. *Undzere Kinder* begins with newsreel shots of children being deported, some with their parents, reminding us at the outset that one of the realities we are about to encounter is the intrusion of such moments, and everything that accompanied them, on the life that lay before them. How will they fare? We are no closer to an answer as the actors, loaded down with mementos of their visit, ride off to their own uncertain prospects. They will remember what they choose to, and forget what they can, making their lives more tolerable in the process. As they disappear, the reprise of the Partisan Song echoes the hopeful opening statement that "this is the generation that freed itself from yesterday's nightmare." It offers us one escape from an age of atrocity that, together with the children, we have managed to survive. But whether its inspiring words restore us to health or lead us to delusion depends on the choice we make between pursuing the path of the daylight or following the road that leads to the realms of the night. And if we follow both, as the film enjoins us to, we are left in a region of twilight wavering between memory and expectation, a dual appeal that offers no easy reconciliation.

TEN

Wiesenthal's *Sunflower* Dilemma
A Response

Simon Wiesenthal's *The Sunflower* need not be read as a personal memoir. It can just as easily be seen as a moral fable invented to illustrate a universal dilemma, even as a version of the parable of the prodigal son, set in the heretical era of the Third Reich. Unlike Elie Wiesel's *Night*, it is not designed to describe Wiesenthal's personal ordeal in the various labor and concentration camps he experienced. We are given few dates and place names; indeed, Wiesenthal never mentions most of the stops on his arduous journey from Lemberg to Mauthausen.

Instead, Wiesenthal offers us two protagonists, two "voices" rather than two characters, in a drama of points of view that remains unresolved to the end. In the narrative a son leaves the family home against his father's wishes to volunteer for the SS and quickly becomes a willing agent of the evil to which that organization is devoted. He is mortally wounded in battle. Unable to reenter his father's house as a penitent or to plead for mercy with his forgotten God, he turns in his final moments to be shriven by a spokesman for the people in whose murder he has taken part—a Jew named Simon Wiesenthal.

There is an overlooked frustrating dimension to this text that makes reading it an exercise in wavering confidence. Some of the premises furnished by Wiesenthal's narrator are questionable, though we have no hint that we are to regard them as anything but the truth. We are told, for example: "Here was a dying man—a murderer who did not want to be a murderer but who had been made into a murderer by a murderous ideology."[1] If the unexamined life is not worth living, unexamined assumptions like these may not be worth writing, unless we are supposed to conclude that we are dealing throughout with a naive narrator whose reactions we cannot trust—and I suspect this was not Wiesenthal's intention. But then we are left with the feeble excuse, offered not by the SS man but by Wiesenthal's narrator, that an ideology rather than individual men was responsible for the slaughter of European Jewry. As presented in the text, Wiesenthal's SS man is an involuntary killer, driven by abnormal circumstances to a deed contrary to his essential beliefs. Such untested inferences abound in *The Sunflower,* making it a far more complicated narrative to interpret than responders to its central dilemma have hitherto acknowledged.

The question of verisimilitude, to say nothing of reliability, cannot be ignored. A man on the verge of death continues a lengthy monologue with scarcely a pause, while his auditor records in memory his exact words, to deliver them more or less verbatim years after the war. We are even expected to accept the unlikely possibility that without having written them down the narrator later recalled the name and address of the SS man's mother, which he had glimpsed briefly only once on the bundle containing his possessions. At their subsequent meeting, the mother gives to Wiesenthal, a total stranger, particulars about her family life as if she were speaking with an old friend. As with her son, Wiesenthal merely listens; the two episodes are parallel monologues in *The Sunflower,* fashioned to establish contrasting portraits of the SS man, forcing us to ask how this child could possibly have been father to that man. We are expected to accept as a given Wiesenthal's ability to recover the language of the mother's monologue decades after the meeting. Details like these, seemingly more convenient than true, are necessary for the narrative, but their presence make us even less certain that *The Sunflower* should be read purely as autobiographical memoir.

I offer these remarks not to criticize Wiesenthal's provocative text but to clarify the terms on which its central crisis should be approached. It is one thing to ask whether an Adolf Eichmann or a Klaus Barbie, after publicly professing what sounds like genuine contrition, deserves spiritual pardon for his deeds. It is another to create an anonymous SS man who after privately acknowledging to a Jewish stranger his participation in an atrocity against Jews, asks forgiveness so that he may die in peace. One virtue of the improbable extralegal setting is that it invites the theoretical inquiry into the implications of the encounter that Wiesenthal's publisher inspired by asking some world-renowned figures to "express an opinion on the moral issue posed in the story"—should Simon Wiesenthal have forgiven the SS man? In the text he did not—he simply listened, and left in silence.

In many respects, the resulting printed Symposium is more challenging than the text itself. When *The Sunflower* appeared in its German edition in 1969, no fewer than twenty-seven respondents sent in opinions. For the first American edition a year later, five new names were added to the list. In 1976 Schocken published a revised American edition deleting some of the original contributors and including several new ones. The variety of reactions reveals not only a diversity of attitudes toward the question of "forgiving" Nazi crimes but also the difficulty of separating one's personal value system from the deeds of the individual being judged. For example, philosophers Herbert Marcuse and Jacques Maritain each submitted only a few paragraphs, but their stances could not have been more contrary: "I believe that the easy forgiving of such crimes," Marcuse tersely wrote, "perpetuates the very evil it wants to alleviate." Maritain, in contrast, furnished Wiesenthal with the proper formula for answering the SS man's request: "'What you have done,' Wiesenthal should have said, 'is, humanly speaking, unforgivable. But *in the name of your God,* yes, I forgive you.'" He then hastened to remind Wiesenthal that there was yet time to restore the health of his *own* soul: "I think you are still in a position to perform this act of charity now, in prayer and before God (all moments of time being present in divine eternity), and that this will put your conscience at rest" (170, 171).

Like most of the contributors to the Symposium, Maritain admits that no one can forgive a killer for atrocities committed against another, but like Dostoyevsky he subscribes to a hierarchy that places compassion above justice on the scale of human merit. It is a little disheartening to see how often in these replies the focus of discussion shifts away from the crimes of the SS man to Wiesenthal's silent response, as if a burden of latent guilt lay equally on the consciences of the killer and the victim. The most extreme expression of this attitude, a truly staggering (and, some might argue, utterly insensitive) conclusion comes from Edward A. Flannery, a member of the Catholic Bishops' Secretariat for Catholic-Jewish Relations. Father Flannery ends his reasoning as follows: "while conscious of the vast differences in the respective situations and culpabilities involved, we may ask whether Simon [Wiesenthal] and his advisors did not themselves participate in Karl's [the SS man's] sin" (115).

The tendency to shelve the evil of the particular deed in the sanctuary of religious doctrine—here, original sin—will seem harsh, one hopes, to more than Jewish readers of *The Sunflower* and its 1976 Symposium. Gustav W. Heinemann, at the time of his answer president of the Federal Republic of Germany, similarly sweeps behind the door of formal theology the debris that still cluttered the memory of his nation: "Justice and Law, however essential they are, cannot exist without Forgiveness. That is the quality that Jesus Christ added to Justice and with which He gave his life" (129–130). Preaching to the unconverted, to say nothing of the believers, must have seemed singularly inappropriate to those struggling with the enigma of why Heinemann's dogma of faith had been so ineffectual *during* the era of the Third Reich, when it was most needed.

Abraham J. Heschel joined a host of other commentators with his conviction that "no one can forgive crimes committed [against] other people." But he dissociated himself from the orthodox Christian view more concretely by adding: "According to Jewish tradition, even God Himself can only forgive sins committed against Himself, not man" (131). Heschel thus alters the terms of the dialogue, inviting us to ask who is to speak on behalf of the millions of murdered and how to assess the "guilty" for a crime of such magnitude.

Primo Levi, along with Jean Améry the only actual survivor of a deathcamp to offer a comment—we do not know how many others, if any, were asked—was familiar with SS men through their actions, not their imputed repentance, so is naturally skeptical of the portrait Wiesenthal draws. Why more readers did not pursue his reasoning remains a mystery, unless we are to believe that people in general prefer to accept the best, even about mass murderers, in order to protect the stability of their own moral and spiritual lives. Levi wrote: "The figure of the SS man as portrayed in your book does not appear as fully reinstated from the moral point of view. Everything would lead one to believe that, had it not been for his fear of impending death, he would have behaved quite otherwise." A strong sense of reality drove Levi to doubt not only the sincerity but the value of a remorse that came too late for those who might still be alive had it come earlier. Levi is virtually the only one (Nechama Tec will join him in a later response) to charge Karl with selfishness: "his action, examined in depth, is tinged with egoism, since one detects in it an attempt to load onto another one's own anguish" (162).

If few others shared Levi's view, we can perhaps attribute this in part to an eager if naive desire to find seeds of virtue in the bleakest display of evil. An unrepentant SS man would threaten the foundations of the civilization in which most members of the Symposium thrive, to say nothing of their audience. Knowing the nature of SS killers, Levi could not take Wiesenthal's question seriously; even if Wiesenthal had granted forgiveness, Levi wryly observes, "it would have been an empty formula and consequently a lie" (162).

This view is in such sharp contrast to the one presented by Jacob Kaplan, chief rabbi of France, that the two seem to inhabit alien spheres of thought. Because Rabbi Kaplan assumes (as Levi was never able to bring himself to do, having watched the SS at work) that Wiesenthal's Karl differs from the others because he "bitterly regrets his crimes and . . . accepts as a just punishment the cruel suffering inflicted by his wounds," he is able to draw the situation into the insulated orbit of his own belief without exposing himself to the deeper problem of the real suffering inflicted by the SS man's *crime.* The rabbi revels instead in his transfigured version of the "former" criminal, with no evidence other than the surface text to justify his claim: "This SS man was not one of those who experienced a sadistic joy in torturing the Jews. *He bore them no hatred* [emphasis mine]. He even felt compassion for what they were suffering" (143). Utterly lost in this admiration is Karl's prior willingness to burn Jews alive and to shoot those who leapt from the blazing building. Even if it were true, as Rabbi Kaplan insists, that Karl's "remorse gave him no respite," this does not deliver us from the more challenging scrutiny of why he was willing to engage in mass murder in the first place.

One of the most surprising discoveries of the Symposium is the ease with which so many commentators allow the SS man to escape *inwardly* from the consequences of his atrocity. Legal expert Milton Konvitz is content to reduce Karl's status to Kantian categories, thereby affirming a continuity in the standards by which we view such appalling cruelty. He writes, somewhat melodramatically but with a tranquil spirit: "what we have in *The Sunflower* is a man writhing in physical and spiritual agony, on the verge of death, filled with painful remorse. He is suffering what Kant called natural punishment" (159–160). Kant wrote that in natural punishment, vice punished itself, and this neat equation allows us to dismiss any possible differences between the unnatural crimes of the Nazis and the natural vices that most flesh is heir to. Kant, after all, never heard of the Holocaust. A bold leap into a realm where the familiar signposts have been shattered and we are left wandering in a moral landscape without guidance proves unappealing to most members of this Symposium.

What is the reason for this? Why, a quarter-century after the event, were so many leading thinkers still content to analyze Wiesenthal's question in utterly conventional terms, ignoring the viewpoint of the tiny minority embodied in British journalist Terrence Prittie's succinct reply: "I find the idea of a mock-forgiveness of a man who helped to burn women and children alive repellent"? Even a respondent who herself had suffered in a Gestapo prison, German writer Luise Rinser, cannot bring herself to condemn her countryman outright. Indeed, she pursues the dubious reasoning that Wiesenthal shares guilt equally with Karl, because the SS man "had acted in ignorance" (a quaint and ancient Socratic argument about the sources of evil conduct) while "you were acting with your eyes open" (194, 195).

Thus mass murder and failure to forgive become interchangeable feats, in Rinser's idiosyncratic view the failure to forgive to be judged more severely than mass murder. Reproaching the innocent has become a pastime for more than one well-known Holocaust commentator, though none to my knowledge has quite reached the level of condemnation that falls so lightly from Rinser's lips: "I shudder at the thought that you let that *repentant* young man go to his death without a word of forgiveness"! If a victim of the Nazi regime, a non-Jew, to be sure, can reach this "enlightened" notion without misgivings, can censure the Jewish Wiesenthal for his indifference to suffering and describe her SS compatriot as a young man "led astray by Nazi ideology" who "thought he was acting rightly when he killed Jews" and thus has on his side the principle in moral theology that "there is a right in mistaken conscience" (198, 197)—if such sinister logic can emerge from such an intelligent mind, then perhaps current concepts of mind, morality, and logic are to be rebuked as well as the person in whom they reside.

This is, of course, more than we can expect of a civilization that continues to take pride in the intellectual and philosophical achievements of this triumvirate. Yet the surfeit of piety that saturates so many of the contributions to this Symposium does not begin to give us a clue to the dilemma of how the murder of European Jewry was possible in the middle of the twentieth century. In 1997, soon after the twenty-fifth anniversary of its initial appearance, Schocken gave us a revised version of that work, retaining eleven of the original opinions, adding thirty-four new ones, and including, to the bewilderment and consternation of many readers some tasteless and self-serving observations by Albert Speer, who died in 1981.

We are now more than fifty years from the event, and the new Symposium allows us to ask what changes, if any, have occurred during the interval in response to Wiesenthal's question and to the Holocaust in general. The single most refreshing shift appears in the replies of a newly vocal generation of Christian thinkers whose views were neglected in the previous Symposium. Discontented with the surfeit of piety that infiltrated the opinions of so many of their predecessors, they seem determined to restore to the dialogue an emphasis on punishable crime rather than forgivable sin.

Franklin H. Littell speaks for many of them when he introduces the idea, well-nigh ignored in the first edition of *The Sunflower*, of churchmen "who were either running with the perpetrators or at least complicit spectators of the genocide of the Jews." Although the following charge is explicit in its condemnation, Littell could have omitted the concept "Christian" without violating the relevance of his assault: "The Christian churches have yet to confront the truth that during the Holocaust there opened up a yawning chasm between traditional Christian words and actual Christian actions and inactions."[2] Not only Christian churches but most well-intentioned "outsiders" used traditional language as a *barrier* against direct encounter with the atrocity of mass murder. The surfeit of piety that narrows the discussion of impious crimes to issues of repentance and forgiveness pays homage to familiar vocabulary at the expense of the crimes themselves, that recede into the shadows of forgetfulness.

Eva Fleischner, like Littell a longtime vigorous and original Christian commentator on the Holocaust overlooked in earlier editions of *The Sunflower*, adds another bold innovation to the dialogue by acknowledging the limitations of Wiesenthal's scenario and daring to depart from it. She chides the SS man for being blind to the suffering not of the Jews he has murdered (though there is some of that in his testimony) but of those still alive in the camps and ghettos. This is an approach that addresses the problem of the dying Karl's responsibilities not to his own soul but to Jews like Simon Wiesenthal who are daily threatened with an awful death. "Could Karl," Fleischner asks, "have done something to ameliorate their fate, or the fate of at least a few Jews, by speaking to his fellow SS instead of summoning a poor, helpless, doomed Jew to his bedside" (143)?

Suppose, for example, the SS man had sent for the local commandant of the camp where Wiesenthal and his friends were housed and tried to extract from him a promise to stop persecuting the Jews. An unlikely and probably a futile gesture, to be sure, but a possible one, executed much too late, but indicating Karl's willingness to risk the loss of Nazi "honor" and a "proper" memorial after his death. "Some sins," concedes Mathew Fox, a Catholic and later an Episcopal priest, "are too big for forgiveness, even for priests. Public penance is required" (145). What better penance than for Karl to renounce his loyalty to the goals of the SS before his death in front of his compatriots. *This,* as Eva Fleischner suggests, might have been a genuine act of atonement. But if it ever occurred to Wiesenthal's dying SS man, we learn nothing about it.

Unfortunately, the new Symposium does not reveal a uniformly radical change in point of view. Rabbi Harold S. Kushner's response soars with passionate conviction, but it is a sentimental appeal, shorn of any acknowledgment of the exact nature of the atrocity. "To be forgiven," he writes, "is to feel the weight of the past lifted from our shoulders, to feel the stain of past wrongdoing washed away. To be forgiven is to feel free to step into the future unburdened by the precedent of who we have been and what we have done in previous times" (174). The crime, the criminal, and most of all the victims are swept aside in one grand rhetorical flourish. Admirable and eloquent as all this sounds, and granting that Kushner sees such "being forgiven" as a miracle from God rather than a bestowal by a human being, one winces at the prospect of a Heinrich Himmler or Reinhard Heydrich stepping into the future unburdened by the precedent of who they had been or what they had done in previous times.

Thus Christian respondents are not the only ones indulging in the dubious virtue of a cheap grace. Thankfully, such voices are in a minority in the new Symposium. In many ways the most powerful reaction comes from the one person in either edition of *The*

Sunflower (and this includes Primo Levi and Jean Améry) to have been in the deathcamps himself and to have lost his family there. Moshe Bejski, a justice of the Supreme Court of Israel and a witness at the Eichmann trial, repudiates universalist discourse such as Rabbi Kushner's by arguing that for the survivor of the Holocaust "the emotional state, the severe mental pressure, and the circumstances . . . cannot be reproduced because they have never existed before and because the human mind has never invented anything like them." Any approach to Wiesenthal's question that does not heed and explore the *unprecedented* nature of the event must falter because, according to Bejski, it fails to understand that "circumstances prevented [Wiesenthal] from thinking and reacting in a rational and deliberate manner, based on moral, religious, humanitarian, or philosophical considerations." For Bejski, an expression of forgiveness from Wiesenthal would have meant a "betrayal and repudiation of the memory of millions of innocent victims who were unjustly murdered, among them, the members of his family" (112, 114, 115).

Bejski is one of the few to highlight the crucial role of memory in our response to Wiesenthal's question and to the experience of the Holocaust. In a curious way, forgiveness of the criminal seems to sanction forgetting of the crime, though perhaps only someone like Bejski who outlived the atrocity himself is justified in articulating the subtlety of this affiliation: "The crimes committed by the Nazi regime were so barbarous," he writes, "and so destructive to the victims that those who somehow managed to survive have never been able to free themselves of the horrors they had to endure. . . . Thus, in addition to all their other injustices the Nazis themselves have prevented their crimes from being forgotten. The survivors have been sentenced to bear their pain and sadness to the grave. Without forgetting there can be no forgiving" (116).

Such a sober statement, if we accept it—and I believe the dreadful events of the catastrophe leave us no option—has enormous and wide-ranging implications. The need for a revision, and then a re-vision, of our cherished value systems is the chief spiritual legacy of the Holocaust. The role of humanity and God during and after the disaster, as Father John T. Pawlikowski candidly concedes in his response, requires "a major redefinition of human and Divine agency in the world. God's control and God's interventionist possibilities can no longer be envisioned in the same way as they were in biblical and classical versions of Judaism and Christianity" (214). And neither can humanity's. Despite the conventional phrasing of his question about forgiveness, Simon Wiesenthal's uneasiness about his plight suggests that he may have had a hint of this himself. Some imaginative leaps must bridge too broad a chasm, and for the reader this may have been one of them. Thus the only truly cogent response to Wiesenthal's question may be the approach that begins with a revision, and then a re-vision, of the text of *The Sunflower* itself.

Of all the respondents to both Schocken editions of the narrative, only one disagrees with virtually all of its premises and "rewrites" it to make it consistent with a world ruled by the laws of death. It cannot be accidental that the author is himself a son of survivors who saw sixty-two relatives murdered by Germans much like Wiesenthal's SS man Karl. André Stein is both a professor of human communications and a practicing therapist working with Holocaust survivors. His statement clearly emerges from his familiarity with the daily routine of atrocity that shadowed the life of the victim. This leads him to a simple dismissal of the orthodox terminology that governs so many other contributions to the Symposiums:

> Any a posteriori speculation as to forgiving a dying SS
> murderer is ethically questionable. In the absurd culture
> of the deathcamp where every moment was saturated
> with its own premature ending, all decisions were by

necessity the consequence of planned randomization of meanings. Nothing could be taken for granted on the basis of a previous stock of knowledge. Any act, decision, compliance with an order could as easily be life-affirming as life-threatening. Nothing made sense. The victims were evicted from their own destiny. Often, the result was a trance Simon calls "mental paralysis" in which one's choices were likely to lead to destruction. Since in the concentrationary universe nothing survived intact from the previous lifeworld of the Jew, Simon's silence had to be a choiceless choice; it should not be argued in the lap of ordinary daily reality and with the distance of half a century (236).

A world governed by the "planned randomization of meanings"—it takes some reflection to realize how sinister yet precise this unsettling expression is—is one where "nothing makes sense." Hence by conceiving the encounter between the SS man and himself within the frame of familiar discourse about repentance and forgiveness, Wiesenthal unwittingly restores some potential "sense" to the meeting and a far from random "meaning" to the incident of atrocity that inspired it. By suggesting the limitations of this approach, Stein invites the reader to question many of Wiesenthal's assumptions and to embark on an inquiry that breaches the boundaries of traditional thought and ventures into terrain implied but left unexplored by the text. This counter-response to the narrative in *The Sunflower,* so deftly outlined by André Stein, is a valuable if solitary reading that merits wider attention.

Curiously, of the eleven contributors who appear in both Symposiums, only one felt the need to revise the earlier submission. In his first essay, Father Edward H. Flannery had ended with the shocking query "whether Simon and his advisors did not themselves participate in Karl's sin," allowing theological considerations to shrink if not eliminate the difference between the criminal and his victims. Whether through the passage of time or the intervention of Vatican III or simply a change of outlook, Father Flannery now offers a far more flexible interpretation, sensitive to the dilemma of Simon and his fellow Jewish prisoners. He drops his charges of complicity and replaces them with a prayer for the SS man's soul "and for those of the victims of his inhuman behavior" (138). Even more to his credit, he adds a possibility unmentioned in his original version: though he still personally subscribes to the "universality and permanence of basic moral laws" (137), he admits that other "religious, ethical and ideological premises" sometimes mandate—the case of the Holocaust would be one example—that moral norms be relativized in recognition of changing "individual and social needs and desires" (138). Perhaps subsequent widely publicized and well-documented atrocities in places like Cambodia, Rwanda, and Bosnia, all acknowledged in particular replies in the later Symposium, have led to a broader and more charitable outlook toward the complex relation between victims and criminals.

By far the most enigmatic presence in the new Symposium is Albert Speer, a convicted war criminal who slyly surfaces as a subtle successor to Simon Wiesenthal's other partner in the ritual of forgiveness, the SS man Karl. No other explanation for Speer's inclusion in the Symposium seems plausible. His contribution could not have been written for the later edition and had not been written for the earlier one; it seems to have been plucked from an intermediate version published in Germany. Speer builds his remarks upon a letter he sent to Wiesenthal after meeting with him in 1975. In Wiesenthal's text we have no hint of what might have happened to the relationship if Karl had survived and Wiesenthal had forgiven him. Speer's extract is a kind of coda to the events of *The Sunflower;* it transforms him into a repentant hero and Wiesenthal into a forgiving one, ennobling both, resolving Simon's dilemma, and introducing the possibility of closure to the nagging question of how victim and criminal can overcome the burdens of their unmastered past. And though only Speer describes the confrontation, unless he is exaggerating Wiesenthal himself must have assented to the accuracy of his account.

The danger for uninitiated readers is that they may be beguiled by Speer's orchestrated version of his response to the Third Reich, in whose closing years he served as minister of armaments (and hence approved the use of slave labor in factories and mines, where thousands died from abuse and starvation). In addition, though Speer begins his excerpt with the confession "Afflicted by unspeakable suffering, horrified by the torments of millions of human beings, I acknowledged responsibility for these crimes [which included the murder of the Jews] at the Nuremberg Trial" (231), he does not add that at Nuremberg he also denied *knowing* about the fate of the Jews until the time of the trial. Of course he was lying, though conclusive proof of this did not emerge until long after Nuremberg. But his moral posture was so distinct from the constant denials of other leading Nazis in the dock that, according to many historians, it impressed some of his judges enough to save him from the hangman's noose.

Anyone familiar with the extensive Holocaust commentary available to us, whether by scholars or others, will know how much of it contains, often unwittingly, a dimension of self-portraiture. The question, as in all forms of autobiography, is how trustworthy are our narratives about ourselves, especially since our self-portraits become portraits for the world to remember us by after we are gone. This is especially true for a man with a history such as Speer's. He fairly grovels with gratitude for the benediction he says Wiesenthal bestowed on him, though his words betray an uncanny ventriloquism as they leap from the page while his voice merges with the silenced speech of the dead SS man: "You showed clemency, humanity, and goodness when we sat facing one another. . . . You did not touch my wounds. You carefully tried to help. You didn't reproach me or confront me with your anger." Speer thus becomes a spokesman for all his compatriots who contributed to the murderous work of a criminal regime, while Simon Wiesenthal appears as the agent of a forgiving world community whose "eyes are not filled with hatred; they remain warm and tolerant and full of sympathy for the misery of others." For whom was Wiesenthal speaking when he wrote in Speer's copy of *The Sunflower* "that I [that is, Speer] did not repress that ruthless time, but had recognized it responsibly in its true dimensions" (231, 232)? Though Speer now feels touched by God's grace, few other respondents to the Symposium would greet this simple-minded ceremony of absolution with unrestrained applause.

For what, after all, can "recognized it responsibly in its true dimensions" mean from the lips of a man who risked his life in the closing days of the war by flying into a beleaguered Berlin to say goodbye to his beloved Führer? We need to learn from Wiesenthal himself why he would hunt down an Eichmann but forgive a Speer—if indeed this is what his actions were meant to convey. Apparently he lightened Speer's burden by agreeing to meet him face-to-face; if Speer's evidence is to be trusted, he also lightened his own, answering his question at the end of *The Sunflower* and in the process undermining some of its ambiguous force. A third Symposium will not be needed.

As for myself, I have no idea what I might have done in Simon Wiesenthal's place, nor do I believe that the question is a legitimate one. Role-playing about Holocaust reality trivializes the serious issues of judgment and forgiveness that *The Sunflower* raises. In my opinion, discussion should focus on the SS man's request and Wiesenthal's original response to it.

The mass murder of European Jewry is an unforgivable crime. By his own description, the SS man provides the details: Jewish men, women, and children are herded into a building, grenades are thrown in, setting it on fire; the SS men then shoot Jews—

including little children—trying to escape the flames through exits or by jumping from windows. *Can* one repent such a monstrous deed? I do not see how. The real test of the SS man's spiritual integrity came at the moment he received the order to shoot. At that instant he was still a morally free man (assuming he had not taken part in earlier murders). By agreeing to shoot instead of heeding an inner monitor or higher authority and disobeying the order—difficult as that may have been, in his situation—he failed the test and permanently cut himself off from the possibility of forgiveness. This may not be true for other crimes—but the mass murder of European Jewry is not an ordinary crime.

No matter what the criminals—the men and women who planned, authorized, collaborated in, and carried out such atrocities—say or do afterward, the crime of the Holocaust remains unforgivable. How can a criminal be forgiven for an unforgivable crime? It seems to me that in refusing to extend forgiveness to the culprit, Wiesenthal unconsciously acknowledged the indissoluble bond fusing the criminal to that kind of crime. Although many have hailed the sincerity of the SS man's repentance, we have no way of verifying this. All we have is Wiesenthal's remembered account, a reproduced voice, not an authentic one. The long monologues of the dying SS man cannot be verbatim, only approximate; indeed, as I have suggested, they may not reflect an actual event. Hence, the mystery of his inner feelings remains swathed in the bandages that encase his head. Wiesenthal does not enter into a dialogue with him, which might have revealed much; he only listens.

He does carry on dialogues with his fellow Jews, and with a seminarian named Bolek. These dialogues give us an important clue to the dilemma we are facing: the *language* of the exchanges does more to shape our attitude toward the SS man's request for forgiveness than the actual crime he has committed. For example, Bolek understandably chastises Wiesenthal for his failure to forgive: "Whom had the SS man to turn to? None of those he had wronged were still alive?"[3] When we call the murder of helpless Jewish parents and children a "wrong," we ease the crime into the realm of daily forgivable transgressions and relieve ourselves of the burden of facing its utter horror.

Consciously or not, Wiesenthal fills Bolek's mouth with questionable platitudes: "When one is face to face with death one doesn't lie"; "he had no opportunity to expiate the sins which he had committed"; he showed "genuine, sincere repentance for his misdeeds" (84). I believe that anyone capable of labeling the murder of defenseless Jews a "misdeed" sacrifices his right to comment on the subject. Trapped by his theological word-horde, the novice weaves around the by-now unmentioned details of the crime a verbal tapestry of acquittal that shifts the onus of responsibility from the criminal to the victim. Of course, Wiesenthal and not Bolek records these words for the reader, and this raises a problem of narrative authority in the text of *The Sunflower*, alluded to earlier, that would require extensive separate investigation. Certainly most of the book's incidents do not flow naturally from setting and character but are transparently manipulated by the author.

The "disappearing criminal" is one of the most dangerous and lamentable legacies of the Holocaust experience. Ironically, in asking forgiveness of a Jew, the SS man transfers the weight of moral decision from himself to one of his potential victims. This dynamic, unfortunately, recurs in numerous testimonies of Holocaust survivors who, in the absence of real malefactors like the dying SS man, sometimes blame *themselves* for acts or consequences of which they are perfectly innocent. For me, the SS man's request betrays his utter failure to understand the nature of his crime: it seems a desperate last gesture to escape his guilt, though we will never know what his buried motives were. He may not know them himself. Wiesenthal leaves unexamined his SS man's infamous statement that "those Jews died quickly, they did not suffer as I do" (56)—as if being burned alive were a form of merciful death. This statement alone would be enough to indict his sincerity.

Words like "wrong" and "misdeed" grew up in a universe of discourse oblivious to places like Auschwitz and Majdanek, where gas chambers and crematoria flourished. The long list of exempting terms that appear in *The Sunflower*—atonement and expiation, repentance and absolution, confession and forgiveness—reflects a valiant but misguided and ultimately doomed effort to reclaim for a familiar vocabulary an event that has burst the frame of conventional judgmental language. Jean Améry's classic study of his ordeal under Gestapo torture and in Auschwitz, *At the Mind's Limits,* had for its original German title *Jenseits von Schuld und Sühne* (*Beyond Guilt and Atonement*). Améry not only promotes Nietzsche's *Beyond Good and Evil* (*Jenseits von Gut und Böse*) to modern times but also invites us to reconsider the terminology with which we will evaluate the most hideous crime of the twentieth century.

Deep in the bowels of Dante's *Inferno* are a few sinners whose presence must have confounded his contemporary readers, because they believed that these sinners were still alive. In fact, they were; but Dante the poet invents the heretical idea of acts so vicious that they condemn the soul of the sinner to eternal damnation *before* physical death. Hence, the possibility of an unrepentable and thus unpardonable crime is not a new one, though Dante could not have known how this quirk in his orderly design for Hell might herald our current threatening impasse about atrocities that are beyond guilt and atonement.[4]

Imagine an SS man today standing by the remains of a mass grave at Chelmno or Babi Yar and saying, "I'm sorry; I repent what I have done." His words would drift down among the hundreds of thousands of wasted corpses or their ashes, and then sink further, to that lower place where they would echo amid the unforgiven and unforgivable spirits of those eternally damned for having consented to these monstrous acts to begin with. That is where our search for guilt ought to begin—and end.

The Sunflower should prompt us—has always prodded me—to shift the locus of our discussion. The vital question to ask about this text is not whether Wiesenthal should have forgiven the SS man. It is rather why the SS man, as a young boy, against his father's wishes, joined enthusiastically in the activities of the Hitler Youth; why, again presumably against his father's wishes, he *volunteered* for the SS (as free a choice as a man could make at the time); why he then pursued a career in that murderous league of killers without protest, including the episode he tells of on his deathbed; and most important, why he had to wait until he was dying to feel the time had come for repentance and forgiveness. On these issues, the SS man is deftly silent.

A second and more troublesome issue is why Wiesenthal and most of his commentators—there is only one exception—celebrate as an act of supreme virtue the single gesture for which I would censure Wiesenthal myself—his refusal to disabuse the SS man's mother about the true nature of her son's activities during the war. If all survivors, and the Allied forces, had done the same thing, then practically the entire female population of the defeated Third Reich would have been able to preserve an untainted memory of their men, hundreds of thousands of whom had taken part in the persecution and murder of helpless victims—Jews, Gypsies, hostages, prisoners of war, and the long list of other groups tormented, often to death, by the Nazi regime. I find it impossible to understand why shielding a person from the evil her nation, including her own son, spread across the face of Europe should be considered an act of *charity*—surely helping her to acknowledge that past and to sort out her own passive role in her nation's guilt would have embodied a greater good.

But an unnecessary one, because the weakest link in Wiesenthal's text is his narrative assumption that such a woman could have endured thirteen years of Nazi rule without having an inkling of the kind of activities the SS were engaged in. All Wiesenthal does is to reinforce the myth of "inner emigration" that allowed many Germans after the war to claim that they knew nothing about their government's criminal projects. Wiesenthal's portrait of a "lonely woman sitting sadly with her memories"—perfectly innocuous ones, it seems—is an unfortunate piece of sentimental excess, seducing us into approving an attitude that would not hold up under rational scrutiny, one marring an otherwise intriguing tale.[5] If every returning victim had behaved so toward the citizens of Nazi Germany, they would have encouraged a general conspiracy of silence dwarfing the protestations of ignorance that did arise, to the dismay of many, after the war. The almost universal acclaim that greeted Wiesenthal's behavior to the mother proves how ill-prepared both language and consciousness remain, fifty years after the event, to grasp and pursue the disruptive consequences of the murder of European Jewry.

As for Wiesenthal, I would prefer at the end to separate the man from his narrative. He is shrewder than his story conveys. He admits it might have been a mistake not to have told the mother the truth. It probably was a mistake to have visited her in the first place. He knows that the daily acts of compassion that grace our lives are insufficient to encompass the enormity of the Holocaust, just as he understands that the burden of forgiveness cannot be his to bear alone. We are not privy to what he really thought or felt about Albert Speer, other than what Speer allows us to hear, just as we are left to conjecture about the SS man's motives beyond what Wiesenthal chooses to disclose. *The Sunflower* is one more arrow shot into the darkness of Holocaust atrocity, and we follow it toward the obscured target of enlightenment with the same tentative impulses that are roused by all other texts on the subject.

ELEVEN

Opening Locked Doors
Reflections on Teaching the Holocaust

Imagine a teacher fifty years from now in a course on the twentieth-century short story trying to introduce a work that begins, "All of us walked around naked" (Tadeusz Borowski, "This Way for the Gas, Ladies and Gentlemen") or "Those who had no papers entitling them to live lined up to die" (Jakov Lind, "Soul of Wood").[1] Indeed, such opening sentences in a course today not expressly named "Holocaust Literature" might rouse the same bewildered initial response that they certainly will in that future short story course. Operations like delousing, deportation, and mass murder do not vibrate with the same imaginative appeal as more familiar social behavior. The need to furnish an explicit context for Holocaust chronicles will increase as the event itself recedes in time and public reminders such as the Holocaust Museum in Washington, D.C., or the film *Schindler's List* become ignored emblems of an earlier era.

Most literature—indeed, most history—does not estrange its readers with startling remarks about a remote way of being. The first words of *Anna Karenina*—"Happy families are all alike"—may not be true, but they strike a comforting note contrary to the anxious images that launch the stories of Borowski and Lind. The sociable moments that define the lives of peasants and gentry in Tolstoy's nineteenth-century Russia—the ball, the wedding, the opera, the salon, the railway journey, mowing, hay-gathering, berry-picking—have no parallel in Holocaust literature. (The rail journey for the Jews was not, as it was for Anna Karenina, a summons to passion but a pathway to death). Readers of this literature find few analogies to ease them into its milieu. The bleak landscape of Holocaust atrocity requires a guide, not to lead us through the patterned horrors of Dante's Hell, where Divine Justice prevails, but into a far more lawless region, where turmoil rules while murderers and their prey share a ruin unlike any we have ever seen before.

Some Kafka critics insist that he foresaw our age of catastrophe, but despite the sinister quivers in his texts, the climate of his fiction is not drenched in the threat of human physical decay that pervades so many Holocaust narratives. For his characters, loss of identity is a greater hazard than loss of life; they find themselves wandering through a maze of bureaucratic officialdom that anyone mindful of the uniformed hierarchies of the Austro-Hungarian Empire will have little trouble recognizing. But those of us who teach the Holocaust search in vain for metaphors of cruelty or antecedents in actual time to cast light on this frightful episode of history. We seem to be left with the challenge of unearthing a context each time we approach this painful subject.

Consider the Polish writer Ida Fink's brief story (three pages long) "The Key Game" from *A Scrap of Time and Other Stories* (1987). We are offered neither date nor locale for the narrative, simply a vague allusion to "the start of the war." The characters have no names—they are merely the man, the woman, and the child. Only slowly do we grasp that they are members of a single family. The opening line gives no clue to the panic-stricken world we are about to enter: "They had just finished supper and the woman had cleared the table, carried the plates to the kitchen, and placed them in the sink." Nothing urgent here: a routine scene of domestic calm. The reader feels safe—but for no more than an instant. The real theme of this story might be called "hiding for your life," and the problem for the author, as for so many other Holocaust writers, is how to lure an audience into the domain of terror that disturbs normal family harmony in this tale. The agitated father and his three-year-old son practice a prescribed ritual, in case "searchers" should come some day when the mother is away at work: the father tries to squeeze into a concealed recess in the bathroom while the son pretends to look for the key to the apartment before he answers the doorbell. No one worries what might happen to the child should the "searchers" believe he is really alone. The words "German" and "Jew" never appear to mark the source of the father's fear. The malefactors are identified only as "searchers" and "the people who would really ring the bell."[2]

Concealment is one of Fink's favorite motifs, and it has strong psychological as well as physical vibrations. The average student of Holocaust literature is unequipped by his or her background to venture into those dark corners of the concealed self that drove so many potential victims to make staying alive the top priority of their menaced existence. Illuminating human behavior under these circumstances, trying to teach about a self constantly in danger of annihilation, is a major test for Holocaust educators. Moreover, narratives featuring heroism, resistance, and spiritual uplift do little to help students enter the veiled space of the concealed self. The deepest atrocities of the Holocaust lie in that shadowy area, where the ruthless German impulse to humiliate their victims temporarily disabled the power of human dignity and drove many survivors to shun the chance to speak about this paralysis even years after the event. One of the most difficult tasks of the teacher is to locate texts that shed some light on this distressing legacy.

It may sound subversive to say so, but Ida Fink's stories are infinitely more valuable in probing this vital topic than Anne

Frank's universally acclaimed *Diary of a Young Girl* (or the mediocre, sentimental drama loosely based on it). Anne Frank was a talented and sensitive adolescent with a promising future as a writer, but her major concern was not the murder of European Jewry, and her vignettes of life in hiding in the secret annex provide a limited vision of the ordeal facing most European Jews in similar situations. Unless we use other narratives to amplify Anne Frank's diary, we are left with a distinctly restricted image of how Jewish families under stress during the Nazi era struggled to preserve a semblance of normalcy.

Only by multiplying voices can we begin to present the moral complexity of the Holocaust experience to individuals accustomed to basing their conduct on stable value systems. The little-known diary of Dawid Sierakowiak, for example, allows us to study tensions unfamiliar to the less immediately threatened dwellers in Anne Frank's secret annex. Sierakowiak, who died of tuberculosis at the age of nineteen in the Lodz ghetto, made daily entries from 1939 until his death on August 8, 1943. His description of the roundup of his own mother in September 1942, along with ten thousand other Jews, including the ill, the aged, and all children under ten (most were shipped to their death), makes Anne Frank's family conflicts seem rather tame: "After my mother's examination and while she was frantically running around the house, begging the doctors to save her life, my father was eating soup. True, he was a bit bewildered, and approached the police and the doctors, but he didn't run outside to beg people he knew in power to intercede on her behalf. In short, he was glad to be rid of a wife with whom life was lately getting too hard, a fact which Mother had to struggle with."[3] Such passages force readers to consider extending the frontiers of moral possibility to include modes of conduct that no one could normally justify.

Holocaust literature taints the imagination with portraits of "impossibilities" like this one, a pathetic rather than a monstrous indifference that even the son cannot sympathize with. He is relentless in his bitter honesty: "My little, exhausted mother, who has suffered so much misfortune and whose life has been one long sacrifice for family and others, would probably not have been taken because of weakness had she not been robbed of food by my father and Nadzia [his sister]" (384). Sierakowiak's diary entries raise vital issues that no serious Holocaust teacher can avoid. In these passages we have an example of what I call the "disappeared criminals," because the only actors in the "drama" are family members. Students who ask how "they" (the persecuted) could have allowed themselves to be mistreated and murdered might without guidance assume that the victims described in Sierakowiak's diary were agents who conspired in their own doom, that the father was somehow responsible for the fate of his wife. So vividly do narratives like Sierakowiak's animate the details of his family's forlorn existence that the deeds of the "disappeared criminals" could easily dissolve in the future into a role defined as "forgotten culprits." Only the constant use of context, chiefly historical, can discourage the uninformed student from leaping to judgment and blaming Sierakowiak's father for the nightmare that consumed his wife and distressed his son. He himself died of starvation soon after.

As we approach the twenty-first century, the need grows more urgent for teachers to achieve a balance between the history of the catastrophe and the various ways of representing the private ordeals of its victims. At the University of Vermont years ago Raul Hilberg established a model (little imitated by other educators) for teaching the subject by joining with a colleague in the English department to offer an interdisciplinary course in the history and literature of the Holocaust. No respectable course or unit on this topic can afford to ignore either discipline. The moral plight of Sierakowiak and his father reflects the impact of inhuman ghetto conditions on traditional family values. His diary is a vital personal and historical document. But fictional stories of the Lodz ghetto by a writer like Isaiah Spiegel are equally vivid.[4] They give flesh to the naked bones of another diary excerpt, written by an anonymous young man in the margins of a French novel. Spiegel's version of ghetto life and the diarist's are really inseparable, pumping life into each other as if blood from the veins of fiction and the arteries of fact flowed in the same body.

Here is an entry from the unknown author's diary:

> What kind of world is this and what kind of people are these who are able to inflict such unbelievable and impossible suffering on living beings?
>
> Our nearest ones have been murdered, some by starvation, some by deportations (modern civilian death). In a manner unheard of in history, we've been crippled physically, spiritually, emotionally—in our whole personality. We vegetate in the most horrible misery and need; we are slaves who, deprived of our own will, feel happy when we're being trodden upon, begging only that we not be trodden to death. I don't exaggerate: we are the most wretched beings the sun has ever seen— and all this is not enough for the "strong man": they continue deporting and tearing our hearts to pieces— while we'd be happy to live even as enslaved, wretched insects, as abject, creeping reptiles—only to live . . . live . . . .[5]

Few passages raise with such concise fervor two key issues that continue to vex our imagination: the inner state of the murderers and the inner state of the victims. It is of course important to understand the mechanics of the Holocaust, the slow but systematic reduction of the Jews to a helpless condition—but that is only the external narrative, which when pursued alone leaves the story incomplete. Students need to explore the dark cave of motive— and without the aid of traditional psychology. Traditional psychology has done little to answer the diarist's plea: "what kind of people are these who are able to inflict such unbelievable and impossible suffering on living beings?" Nor has it explained what happens to the self when its main and often sole driving force is to stay alive, "to live . . . live . . . " despite agony, humiliation, loss, and shame.

Anyone teaching this subject must be willing to confront behavior that cannot be explained by prior notions of why we do what we do. Robert Jay Lifton, in his influential work on Nazi doctors, developed the idea of "doubling" to clarify how "civilized" medical professionals could join in the selection of men, women, and children for death in the gas chamber.[6] They did this, Lifton alleges, by separating their "Auschwitz self" from their "normal self." Not everyone is happy with this explanation, which may simply reflect an effort to retain value words like "civilized" and "professional" in our vocabulary of how decent human beings live.[7] An alternate but much less flattering interpretation of the Nazi doctors' conduct is that the majority of them saw selection and brutal experimentation on helpless victims as an *expression* of their values, and hence of their "normal" selves, because they believed that a chief aim of their duty as physicians was to support the goals of Nazi racial ideology. Certainly there was no surplus of public contrition and repentance, to say nothing of penance, among culpable doctors—or any other professionals in Germany—after its defeat in 1945. Many teachers may be daunted by the challenge of inviting students to revise their premises about "reasonable" behavior during the Holocaust by admitting that what we consider evil conduct could be as psychologically rewarding for certain people as charity and love are for the rest of us. Hence reading and teaching Holocaust literature requires a flexible stamina—one might even say courage—that few other subjects require.

Charlotte Delbo writes in *None of Us Will Return* that the unsuspecting new arrivals at Auschwitz may have known the worst but did not know the unthinkable—by which she meant the doom that awaited most of them in the gas chamber.[8] This is the crux of the dilemma facing any Holocaust teacher: Delbo's distinction affronts the moral imagination, eternally unprepared for such a grim possibility. As we teach and study the Holocaust, the unthinkable in its numerous guises clamors to burst into the safe havens of our sedated minds. There, terms like "guilt" and "conscience" have for centuries helped us to array acts of good and evil in separate ranks and judge them accordingly. Then we encounter from a different source an episode like the following, not at all an isolated example of what Delbo meant by "unthinkable," and we are left stunned and wondering how neat categories like guilt or conscience or doubling can explain such behavior. As it happens, the agent is a German doctor named Aribert Heim:

> Dr. Heim came to the Mauthausen concentration camp after completing his medical studies to gain surgical experience in preparation for later duty as front-line medical officer. During his less than a year's time in Mauthausen, 540 inmates were used as guinea pigs and operated to death by him. This "Sonderbehandlung" (special treatment) included amputating the arms or legs of healthy prisoners and cutting open abdomens and then leaving his victims to die without further treatment. After examining the teeth of the prisoners from one transport to the camp, Heim selected two young men with complete sets of teeth, took them to his office and killed them with an injection of poison. He then personally decapitated the corpses, had the heads boiled and cleaned, and finally decorated his desk with one of the skulls, giving the other to a colleague friend of his.[9]

It would be consoling to be able to account for such action by labeling Dr. Heim a lunatic disguised as a physician, but there is no proof to justify this conclusion. On the contrary, Dr. Heim went on to serve as medical officer to an elite SS division. After the war, he turned up as a gynecological specialist in Mannheim. He married another doctor and moved to Baden-Baden, where he and his wife opened a practice. Only years later was he forced to flee Germany, when investigators turned up evidence of his war crimes. He died of cancer in Argentina, easy in conscience if not in body.

Had Dr. Heim been able to view his victims as individuals rather than members of an outcast racial group, he might have had some qualms about his experiments. But both training and ideology had prepared him to classify his subjects as guinea pigs rather than human beings, and the ease with which he managed this must give any educator—indeed, any civilized person—pause. The premise that members of the healing profession are inherently morally, emotionally, or philosophically more sensitive than others to human misery proved to be unfounded in the Third Reich. So did the belief that similar professionals like judges, lawyers, and teachers would instinctively refuse to embrace policies that led to the expulsion and death of large segments of their community. Just as we must make a special effort to recapture the features of the "disappeared criminal" in the pages of Holocaust literature, so must we create a distinct kind of portraiture to sketch the anguish of people who have no agency in their fate since their enemy is not a discernible antagonist but a ruthless racial ideology. Because we have not been taught to think in such terms about human behavior, because we have always considered education a tool to empower students to shape their own futures, we have to make clear when teaching *this* subject that it violates but does not permanently invalidate humane values.

In Germany during the Nazi era, mass murder became government policy: officials had to adapt to their new role as killers, while their victims had to adjust in labor, concentration, and deathcamps to the abnormal pressures of staying alive through strategies they would have found inadmissible in more normal times. After the war, both criminals and survivors resumed their lives, though the oppressors like Dr. Heim with far less difficulty than those they oppressed. This is one of the many ironic legacies that make of the Holocaust a narrative without closure and with few cheerful endings.

Teaching and learning about the Holocaust is thus a double journey, a temporary excursion that concludes with the end of a class or a course, and a ceaseless encounter with evil that raises a multitude of unsettling questions about history and human conduct. I have taught students about the subject for nearly thirty years, and incredulity remains a constant factor in their response. "How could human beings have done that to other human beings?" is one of their recurring queries. And the other is: "How could the victims have been so passive? How could they have let them do that to them without fighting back?" Behind both inquiries lies a naïveté about individual behavior and the forces of history that continues to tax the Holocaust educator. I have always believed that students flock to Holocaust courses not because such courses are fashionable but because they have a deep-lying interest in the Final Solution's criminals and victims, so one of my main goals as a teacher of the Holocaust has been to subvert stereotypical thinking: for example, that only sadists could organize and execute an atrocity like the murder of European Jewry or that all victims went unresistingly to their deaths. But perhaps most important in the list of misunderstood matters is the demise of significant choice for inmates in the Nazi deathcamps.

The best education requires constant scrutiny of accepted ideas, to ensure that what we believe is really worthy of our belief and not merely an escape from some of the less pleasant implications of existence in an imperfect world. Though it is untrue that *any* nation might have carried out a program like the Final Solution, given the right circumstances—an untested but often-heard charge that is nothing more than simple speculation—it is equally imprecise to argue that *only* Germany could have executed such a crime.

Moreover, the conclusion that the Jews were easy to kill because by tradition and nature they were a people accustomed to persecution ignores the ease with which the Germans murdered millions of Soviet prisoners of war and hundreds of thousands of Gypsies. Teachers of the Holocaust face the difficult task of spurning "easy" explanations and exploring with their students the ramifications of an event that has been called unprecedented or unique—though even these terms need to be contextually qualified.

Certainly anyone crossing the frontiers of Holocaust atrocity for the first time—and as the years pass, more and more students will belong to this group—*feels* as if he or she is entering a world without precedent. When Ida Fink called her story "The Key Game," she described not only the fearful dilemma of her characters but also the painful journey of her readers, who must use their own "keys" in the various locks of unfamiliar experiences that block entry to the cryptic ordeal of her fictional family. Opening a locked door is one of those metaphorical moments that transcends the limits of this tale. Hiding behind a door can save a life, as we learn from another of Fink's stories. We also know how many doomed people trembled behind locked doors, waiting for the Gestapo to break in. In "The Key Game," we are asked to stand on both sides of the door, looking in and looking out, thereby multiplying the points of view. How else are we to penetrate this grotesque reality? As we occupy the landscape of the catastrophe we call the Holocaust, we are tugged in two directions at once, prompted to identify with victims like the boy and his family, whose lives are in peril, and to imagine "the people who would really ring the bell," those who come to hunt human prey for reasons we may never understand.

The basic challenge for Holocaust educators is to begin by expanding their own sympathies and vision to include the personalities of all those involved in the disaster—criminals, victims, collaborators, and bystanders—and then gradually to extend to their students means for crossing the threshold into their historical and psychological space. Traditionally, teachers open doors of possibility for their students. In this one instance, they are obliged to open doors of impossibility, an equally compelling but more arduous task, because the obstacles to gaining entrance are so many, the usual rewards so few.

Notes

ONE
Preempting the Holocaust

1. Tape T-662, testimony of Charles A., Fortunoff Video Archive for Holocaust Testimonies at Yale University.
2. Ana Novac, *The Beautiful Days of My Youth: My Six Months in Auschwitz and Plaszow* trans. George L. Newman (New York: Henry Holt, 1997), 158–159.
3. Tzvetan Todorov, *Facing the Extreme: Moral Life in the Concentration Camps,* trans. Arthur Denner and Abigail Pollak (New York: Henry Holt, 1996), 36–37, 121.
4. Judy Chicago, *Holocaust Project: From Darkness into Light* (New York: Viking, 1993), 5.
5. Todorov, *Facing the Extreme,* 258.
6. Chicago, *Holocaust Project,* 11, 9, 10.
7. Eugene Borowitz and Frans Jozef van Beeck, "The Holocaust and Meaning: An Exchange," *Cross Currents* 42 (Fall 1992): 420.
8. Frans Jozef van Beeck, "Two Kind Jewish Men: A Sermon in Memory of the Shoa," *Cross Currents* 42 (Summer 1992): 180, 181.
9. Tape T-48, testimony of Paul D., Fortunoff Video Archive.
10. Borowitz and van Beeck, "Holocaust and Meaning," 421, 423.
11. Van Beeck, "Two Kind Jewish Men," 176.
12. Theo Richmond, *Konin: A Quest* (New York: Pantheon, 1995), 479, 480.

TWO
Legacy in Gray

1. Ferdinando Camon, *Conversations with Primo Levi,* trans. John Shepley (Marlboro, Vt.: Marlboro, 1989), 21–22.

2. See Primo Levi, *Survival in Auschwitz: The Nazi Assault on Humanity,* trans. Stuart Woolf (New York: Collier, 1993), 92.
3. Primo Levi, "The Gypsy," in Levi, *Moments of Reprieve,* trans. Ruth Feldman (New York: Summit, 1986), 69.
4. Levi, "A Disciple," in ibid., 52.
5. Levi, "The Gypsy," in ibid., 67.
6. Primo Levi, *The Reawakening: A Liberated Prisoner's Long March Home Through East Europe,* trans. Stuart Woolf (Boston: Little, Brown, 1965), 13.
7. Levi, *Survival in Auschwitz,* 38.
8. Primo Levi, *The Drowned and the Saved,* trans. Raymond Rosenthal (New York: Simon and Schuster, 1988), 48–49.
9. See James Atlas, "The Survivor's Suicide," *Vanity Fair,* January 1988, 94.

THREE

Gendered Suffering

1. Charlotte Delbo, *Auschwitz and After,* trans. Rosette C. Lamont (New Haven and London: Yale University Press, 1995), 257.
2. Tape T-1154, testimony of Sally H., Fortunoff Video Archive for Holocaust Testimonies at Yale University.
3. Tape T-220, testimony of Joly Z., ibid.
4. Tape T-2045, testimony of Arina B., ibid.
5. Ibid.
6. Ibid.
7. Tape T-66, testimony of Shari B., Fortunoff Video Archive.
8. Tape T-107, testimony of Edith P., ibid.
9. Tape T-192, testimony of Viktor C., ibid.

FOUR

The Alarmed Vision

1. My translation. For another version of this poem, as well as others by Dan Pagis, see *Points of Departure,* trans. Stephen Mitchell (Philadelphia: Jewish Publication Society of America, 1981).
2. A main thrust of Pagis's poem is that what Harold Bloom calls the "anxiety of influence" now works in two directions. Hebrew litera-

ture of catastrophe continues to shape subsequent writing in that tradition, but the Holocaust and the "deportation" of Abel and Eve forces on the literary imagination a re-visioning and hence a revisioning of Scripture. Holocaust and Scripture now conspire to alter each other's texts.

3. This episode is recounted in Claude Lanzmann's film *Shoah* by one of the two survivors of the Chelmno deathcamp. Similar narratives may be found in Martin Gilbert, *Holocaust: A History of the Jews of Europe during the Second World War* (New York: Holt, Rinehart and Winston, 1985); Charlotte Delbo's trilogy *Auschwitz and After,* trans. Rosette C. Lamont (New Haven and London: Yale University Press, 1995), esp. vol. 1, *None of Us Will Return;* and Lawrence L. Langer, *Holocaust Testimonies: The Ruins of Memory* (New Haven and London: Yale University Press, 1991). A comprehensive history of the Auschwitz deathcamp is *Anatomy of the Auschwitz Death Camp,* ed. Yisrael Gutman and Michael Berenbaum (Bloomington: Indiana University Press, 1994). For further details about the killing facilities, see Yitzhak Arad, *Belzec, Sobibor, Treblinka: The Operation Reinhard Death Camps* (Bloomington: Indiana University Press, 1987). The full story of the Riegner telegram and the U.S. State Department response may be found in David S. Wyman, *The Abandonment of the Jews: America and the Holocaust, 1941–1945* (New York: Pantheon, 1984). In addition to the failure to imagine the disaster threatening European Jewry, Wyman lists Roosevelt's fear of alienating non-Jewish supporters as well as antisemitism among higher echelons of State Department officials as reasons for the sluggish response to the Jewish situation. The public, too, including parts of the American Jewish community, did not view with enthusiasm an expanded immigration policy during years of lingering economic depression.

4. See Walter Laqueur, *The Terrible Secret: Suppression of the Truth About Hitler's "Final Solution"* (Boston: Little, Brown, 1981), and Walter Laqueur and Richard Breitman, *Breaking the Silence* (New York: Simon and Schuster, 1988). Of course, even if Riegner could have provided intimate details of atrocity to convey the visceral horrors of the Final Solution, his more precise reports still might have been translated by the bureaucracy in Washington into technical memos shuffled from office to office, as was done with his original telegrams. The mentality prevailing in the State Department seemed

more interested in managing the story than in responding to it with some form of prompt action.

5. Karski tells part of his story in Lanzmann's film *Shoah*. The full narrative appears (well before the end of World War II, it should be noted) in Jan Karski, *Story of a Secret State* (Boston: Houghton Mifflin, 1944).

6. Abraham Lewin, *A Cup of Tears: A Diary of the Warsaw Ghetto*, ed. Antony Polonsky, trans. Christopher Hutton (New York: Basil Blackwell, 1989), 236–237. These questions are dated January 9, 1943, one week before the last entry in the Diary, when Lewin and his daughter were presumably rounded up and deported to their death in Treblinka. Haim Nahman Bialik (1873–1934) was the leading poet of the modern Hebrew revival. His "In the Town [or City] of Slaughter" was a response to the Kishinev pogrom in tsarist Russia in 1903, when forty-nine Jews were killed.

7. Perhaps the greatest threat of all to the stage on which we enact our existence is that behind the curtain, nothing exists. But few of us are willing to contend with the possibility of meaninglessness in our lives.

8. For a detailed discussion of the influence of traditional Jewish catastrophe writings on later Holocaust literature, see David G. Roskies, *Against the Apocalypse: Responses to Catastrophe in Modern Jewish Culture* (Cambridge, Mass.: Harvard University Press, 1984). Roskies argues that a direct line leads from one to the other, allowing for no permanent ideational rupture between, for example, depictions of pogroms and depictions of the destruction of European Jewry during World War II. All such efforts have common roots in a literature of lamentation. For an alternate point of view, see Lawrence L. Langer, *The Holocaust and the Literary Imagination* (New Haven and London: Yale University Press, 1975).

9. The question of "survivor guilt" continues to haunt us like a ghost that will not die. The psychological community, especially in America, has made the idea an unchallenged premise about the survival experience. But in an unpublished paper presented at a conference sponsored by the U.S. Holocaust Memorial Museum Research Center in December 1993, Norwegian psychiatrist and Auschwitz survivor Leo Eitinger argued that "most survivors had the same self-reproaches one can hear in all cases of losses: 'If I had done this

or that or if I had not done this or that, perhaps he or she would have lived today.'" Such "guilt," which Eitinger prefers to call self-reproach, is not specific to survivors but represents a common human response. Psychiatrist Anna Ornstein, also a Holocaust survivor, shrewdly refines this idea: "The frequently cited guilt in survivors, I believe, may not be related to having survived while others had died, but rather to the survivors' difficulty in reconciling their behavior and moral conduct during the Holocaust with their conduct and behavior under civilized conditions." See her "The Holocaust: Reconstruction and the Establishment of Psychic Continuity," in Arnold Rothstein, ed., *The Reconstruction of Trauma: Its Significance in Clinical Work* (Madison, Conn.: International Universities Press, 1986), 184–185.

10. Composite tape A-67, testimony of Bessie K. and Jacob K., Fortunoff Video Archive for Holocaust Testimony at Yale University.

11. For a detailed discussion of the uniqueness of the Holocaust as an epistemological event (rather than as an illustration of comparative suffering), see Steven T. Katz, *The Holocaust in Historical Context,* Vol. 1: *The Holocaust and Mass Death Before the Modern Age* (New York: Oxford University Press, 1994). The concept of having missed one's "intended destiny" is born of the German intention to murder every living Jew with no exceptions, an intention that distinguishes the Holocaust from other atrocities, such as the ones in Cambodia and Rwanda. As Katz argues, the distinction is between historical events, not the quality or quantity of the suffering.

12. Tape T-1879, Testimony of Judith G., Fortunoff Video Archive.

13. Tape T-938, testimony of George S., ibid.

14. See Timothy W. Ryback, "A Reporter at Large: Evidence of Evil," *New Yorker,* November 15, 1993, 78.

FIVE

Landscapes of Jewish Experience

1. Tape HVT-618, testimony of Samuel Bak, Fortunoff Video Archive for Holocaust Testimonies at Yale University.

2. *Fahrt ins Staublose: Die Gedichte der Nelly Sachs* (Frankfurt: Suhrkamp, 1971), 152, my translation.

3. Quoted by Gisela Dischner, "Zu den Gedichten von Nelly Sachs," in Bengt Holmquist, ed., *Das Buch der Nelly Sachs* (Frankfurt: Suhrkamp, 1966), 354, my translation.

4. See I. Howe and E. Greenberg, eds., *A Treasury of Yiddish Poetry* (New York: Holt, Rinehart and Winston, 1969), 331; translation by Chana Faerstein.

5. *Fahrt ins Staublose,* 76, my translation.

6. See Nelly Sachs, "Anhang zu *Beryll sieht in der Nacht,*" in *Zeichen im Sand: Die szenischen Dichtung der Nelly Sachs* (Frankfurt: Suhrkamp, 1966), 354, my translation.

7. Ibid.

8. *Fahrt ins Staublose,* 288, my translation.

9. See Erwin Panofsky, *The Life and Art of Albrecht Dürer* (Princeton, N.J.: Princeton University Press, 1943), 168.

10. Ibid.

SIX

Two Holocaust Voices

1. Cynthia Ozick, *The Shawl: A Story and a Novella* (New York: Knopf, 1989), 8, 8–9.

2. Art Spiegelman, *Maus II, A Survivor's Tale: And Here My Troubles Began* (New York: Pantheon, 1991), 116.

SEVEN

The Stage of Memory

1. "A Girl's Diary," in Alan Adelson and Robert Lapides, eds., *Lodz Ghetto: Inside a Community Under Siege* (New York: Viking, 1989), 241–242.

2. "A Father's Lament," in ibid., 348–349.

3. "Dawid Sierakowiak's Diary," in ibid., 269–270.

4. Tape T-113, testimony of Nathan A., Fortunoff Video Archive for Holocaust Testimonies at Yale University.

5. Elie Wiesel, "The Death of My Father," in *Legends of Our Time,* trans. Steven Donadio (New York: Holt, Rinehart and Winston, 1968), 1.

6. Elie Wiesel, *Night*, trans. Stella Rodway (1960; New York: Bantam, 1982), 52.

EIGHT
The Inner Life of the Kovno Ghetto

1. Abraham Tory, *Surviving the Holocaust: The Kovno Ghetto Diary*, trans. Jerzy Michalowicz (Cambridge, Mass.: Harvard University Press, 1990), 55.
2. Tape T-984, testimony of Paula G. Fortunoff Video Archive for Holocaust Testimonies at Yale University.
3. Tory, *Surviving the Holocaust*, 45.
4. Dr. Lazar Goldstein-Golden, *From Ghetto Kovno to Dachau*, trans. Max Rosenfeld and ed. Berl Kagan (New York: Esther Goldstein, 1985), 55. Dr. Goldstein had planned a five-volume work on "The Doom of Lithuanian Jewry" but died, according to his editor, leaving only "a heap of brief notes on many subjects." His editor arranged some of them into a "sequential manuscript," taking responsibility for some of the style but insisting that "the thoughts expressed in this book are Dr. Goldstein's completely."
5. Tory, *Surviving the Holocaust*, 195.
6. Ibid., 207.
7. Leib Garfunkel, "The Destruction of Kovno's Jewry," trans. and paraphrased by Alfred Katz (unpublished manuscript, U.S. Holocaust Memorial Museum, Washington, D.C., 1995), 41.
8. Tory, *Surviving the Holocaust*, 209–210.
9. Goldstein-Golden, *From Ghetto Kovno to Dachau*, pp. 57–58.
10. William W. Mishell, *Kaddish for Kovno: Life and Death in a Lithuanian Ghetto, 1941–1945* (Chicago: Chicago Review Press, 1988), 129.
11. See Dov Levin, *Fighting Back: Lithuanian Jewry's Armed Resistance to the Nazis, 1941–1945*, trans. Moshe Kohn and Dina Cohen (London: Holmes and Meier, 1985).
12. Tape T-190, testimony of Shalom S., Fortunoff Video Archive.
13. Ibid., 132.
14. Tory, *Surviving the Holocaust*, 210.
15. Tamar Lazerson, "Diary of Tamar Lazerson," trans. Judith Cohen

(unpublished manuscript, U.S. Holocaust Memorial Museum, Washington, D.C., 1995), 20.

16. Ibid., 23.

NINE
Undzere Kinder

1. The stars of *Undzere Kinder*, Szymon Dzigan and Yisroel Schumacher, were an active comedy team in Yiddish film and theater before the war. They spent the war years in the Soviet Union, returning after the liberation. Like many of the children in the Jewish orphanage in *Undzere Kinder*, Dzigan and Schumacher play themselves. Natan Gross, the film's director, survived the war in Poland, hidden by a Christian family. *Undzere Kinder* was never released in Poland. It premiered at the Eden Theater in Tel Aviv in 1951. For further information on the history of Yiddish film, see J. Hoberman, *Bridge of Light: Yiddish Film Between Two Worlds* (New York: Museum of Modern Art and Schocken, 1991).

TEN
Wiesenthal's *Sunflower* Dilemma

1. Simon Wiesenthal, *The Sunflower* (New York: Schocken, 1976), 56–57.

2. Simon Wiesenthal, *The Sunflower: On the Possibilities and Limits of Forgiveness,* rev. ed., ed. Harry James Cargas and Bonny V. Fetterman (New York: Schocken, 1997), 189–190.

3. Wiesenthal, *Sunflower* (1976), 83.

4. In canto 33, the penultimate one of the *Inferno,* Dante finds himself in the circle of those punished for being treacherous to guests. There he meets Fra Alberigo, who murdered his kinsman Manfred and Manfred's son at a banquet at his home. Dante is surprised to see him in Hell: " 'Oh then,' I said to him, 'you are already dead?' " (ll. 115–116). Alberigo replies: " 'Down to this place a soul is often conveyed / Before it is sent forth by Atropos [i.e., dies].' " (ll. 120–121). He goes on to explain that when a soul sins as his did, " 'A devil displaces it / And governs inside the body until its toll/Of years elapses.' " (ll. 124–127). The apologists for Wiesenthal's SS man seem

unwilling to entertain this possibility. See Robert Pinsky, *The Inferno: A New Verse Translation* (New York: Farrar, Straus and Giroux, 1994).
5. Wiesenthal, *Sunflower* (1976), 95.

ELEVEN

Opening Locked Doors

1. See Tadeusz Borowski, *This Way for the Gas, Ladies and Gentlemen,* trans. Barbara Vedder (New York: Penguin, 1976), and Jakov Lind, *Soul of Wood and Other Stories,* trans. Ralph Manheim (New York: Hill and Wang, 1964).
2. Ida Fink, *A Scrap of Time and Other Stories,* trans. Madeline Levine and Francine Prose (New York: Pantheon, 1987), 35–38.
3. "Dawid Sierakowiak's Diary," in Alan Adelson and Robert Lapides, eds., *Lodz Ghetto: Inside a Community Under Siege* (New York: Viking, 1989), 333. The full diary is now available. See Alan Adelson, ed., and Kamil Turowski, trans., *The Diary of Dawid Sierakowiak: Five Notebooks from the Lodz Ghetto* (New York: Oxford University Press, 1996).
4. For example, see his story "Bread" in Lawrence L. Langer, ed., *Art from the Ashes: A Holocaust Anthology* (New York: Oxford University Press, 1995), 250–256.
5. Adelson and Lapides, eds., *Lodz Ghetto,* 425.
6. See Robert Jay Lifton, *The Nazi Doctors: Medical Killing and the Psychology of Genocide* (New York: Basic Books, 1986), 418–465.
7. See, for example, Berel Lang, *Act and Idea in the Nazi Genocide* (Chicago: University of Chicago Press, 1990), 49–54.
8. Charlotte Delbo, *None of Us Will Return,* trans. John Githens (New York: Grove, 1968).
9. Simon Wiesenthal Documentation Center, Vienna, *Bulletin of Information No. 34,* January 31, 1994, 3–4.